50 *Hikes*

In Eastern Pennsylvania

From the Mason-Dixon Line to
the Poconos and North Mountain

Fourth Edition

TOM THWAITES

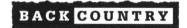

Backcountry Guides

Woodstock, Vermont

AN INVITATION TO THE READER

Over time trails can be rerouted and signs and landmarks altered. If you find that changes have occurred on the routes described in this book, please let us know so that corrections may be made in future editions. The author and publisher also welcome other comments and suggestions. Address all correspondence to:

Editor, 50 Hikes™ Series
Backcountry Guides
P.O. Box 748
Woodstock, VT 05091

LIBRARY OF CONGRESS CATALOGING-IN-PUBLICATION DATA:

Thwaites, Tom.
 50 hikes in eastern Pennsylvania : from the Mason-Dixon Line to the Poconos and North Mountain / Tom Thwaites.--4th ed.
  p. cm.
 Includes index.

 1. Hiking--Pennsylvania--Guidebooks. 2. Backpacking--Pennsylvania--Guidebooks. 3. Trails--Pennsylvania--Guidebooks. 4. Pennsylvania--Guidebooks. I. Title: Fifty Hikes in eastern Pennsylvania. II. Title.

GV199.42.P4T485 2003
917.4804'43--dc21

ISBN-13: 978-0-88150-591-7
ISBN-10: 0-88150-591-9

Cover and interior design by Glenn Suokko

Maps by Richard Widhu and Mapping Specialists Ltd., Madison, WI

Front cover photo of the Delaware Water Gap © Bob Krist/CORBIS

Published by The Countryman Press,
P.O. Box 748, Woodstock, Vermont 05091

Distributed by W.W. Norton & Company, Inc.,
500 Fifth Avenue, New York, NY 10110

Printed in the United States of America

10 9 8 7

50 Hikes in Eastern Pennsylvania

DEDICATION

To Emily and Jeremy Batt, the next generation of hikers

50 Hikes in Eastern Pennsylvania at a Glance

Hike	Location
1. Caledonia State Park	Chambersburg
2. Rocky Knob	South Mountain
3. Pole Steeple	South Mountain
4 Kings Gap	South Mountain
5. York Heritage Trail	York
6. Gifford Pinchot State Park	York
7. Gettysburg	Gettysburg
8. Sunset Rocks	South Mountain
9. Cumberland Valley	Carlisle
10. Joseph E. Ibberson State Conservation Area	Harrisburg
11. Wildwood Lake	Harrisburg
12. Capital Area Greenbelt	Harrisburg
13. Peters Mountain	Harrisburg
14. Stone Tower Trail	Saint Anthony's
15. Swatara State Park	Harrisburg
16. Middle Creek	Reading
17. Susquehannock State Park	Lancaster
18. Nolde Forest	Reading
19. Ridley Creek	Media
20. Skippack Creek Trail	Norristown
21. Wissahickon Gorge	Philadelphia
22. Valley Forge	Norristown
23. Holtwood Recreation Area	Lancaster
24. Tyler State Park	Philadelphia
25. Mill Creek	Reading
26. White Clay Creek	Newark, DE

LENGTH (km)	VERTICAL RISE (m)	VIEWS	GOOD FOR KIDS	CAMPING	X-C SKIING	Notes
4.7	175		★	★		Charcoal iron furnace
6.9	165	★	★			Designated hiking trail
8.7	232	★		★		Appalachian Trail midpoint
10.1	340	★	★			Environmental education center
10.3	none		★			Tunnel
11.1	80		★	★		Large lake & Mason Dixon Trail
13.0	140	★	★			View from Little Round Top, Pickett's Charge
13.3	323	★		★		Appalachian Trail & shelter
16.5	135					Appalachian Trail
4.9	240		★			Appalachian Trail
5.3	20		★			Ole Wine Nature Center
5.5	20		★			Urban greenway
7.6	315	★				Appalachian Trail shelter
12.1	395					Ghost town and mine
18.0	50					Swatara Creek and Waterville bridge
5.3	130	★	★			Wildlife area and visitors center
5.6	220	★	★			Rhododendrons
5.8	146		★			Evergreen plantations
6.9	150		★			An oasis of peace and quiet
7.5	100		★			Low profile state park
7.6	140		★			Covered bridge
7.8	85		★			National park
8.1	250	★	★			Conestoga Trail
8.7	250	★	★			A pleasant walk in the country
10.9	320			★		French Creek State Park
13.6	50		★			An oasis of quiet

50 Hikes in Eastern Pennsylvania at a Glance

Hike	Location
27. The Pinnacle	Hamburg
28. Wilderness Trail	Media
29. Delaware Canal	Easton
30. French Creek State Park	Reading
31. Hawk Falls	Poconos
32. Camelback Mountain	Poconos
33. Skyline Trail	Poconos
34. Blooming Grove Trail	Poconos
35. Mount Minsi	Stroudsburg
36. Dingmans Falls	Poconos
37. Lakeside Trail	Poconos
38. Gouldsboro State Park	Poconos
39. Choke Creek Trail	Poconos
40. Boulder Field	Poconos
41. Pennel Run	Poconos
42. Bruce Lake Natural Area	Poconos
43. Big Bear Swamp	Poconos
44. Promised Land State Park	Poconos
45. Thunder Swamp Trail	Poconos
46. Painter Creek Loop	Poconos
47. Fourth Run Loop	Poconos
48. Frances Slocum	Wilkes-Barre
49. Joe Gmiter	Wilkes-Barre
50. Rickets Glen	North Mountain

LENGTH (km)	VERTICAL RISE (m)	VIEWS	GOOD FOR KIDS	CAMPING	X-C SKIING	Notes
14.0	315	★		★		Camping at Blue Rocks Campground
14.1	245		★			Hike can be truncated; five-dollar admission
17.3	15					Step into transportation history
18.5	353		★			Facilities built by CCC
4.8	135		★	★		Carry kids across stream
6.5	130	★	★			Best view in the Poconos
7.8	215	★	★	★	★	Carry kids across stream
7.9	90		★		★	Trail often rocky, sometimes wet; wear boots
7.9	310	★				Appalachian Trail
8.0	160			★		Camp at Dingmans campground
8.3	25		★	★	★	A mostly paved trail
9.1	91		★	★	★	Camp at Tobyhanna State Park
10.0	90	★				Designated hiking trail
11.3	170		★	★		Edge of the continental ice sheet
11.4	220					Designated hiking trail
11.8	98		★	★	★	Camp at Promised Land State Park
14.2	220			★		Designated hiking trail
14.2	110		★			Large camping area
15.1	250					Designated hiking trail
15.6	280	★				Designated hiking trail
20.0	285			★	★	Ski west of PA 534
5.3	67		★	★		Only PA state park named after a woman
7.2	320					Large state game land
10.7	315			★		Waterfalls in a fun dance

**50 Hikes in
Eastern Pennsylvania**

CONTENTS

V. North Mountain

Acknowledgments

Many of the hikes in this book were suggested by employees of the Pennsylvania Bureau of State Parks, the National Park Service, the Pennsylvania Bureau of Forestry, and members of the Keystone Trails Association.

I thank Oreste Unti, Tom Davidowski, John Seville, Ron Gray, James Becker, James Flandreau, Mike Cosgrove, Erik Williams, Larry Pittis, Joe and Lorraine Healey, Matt Marcinek, Tom Scully, Mark Arbogast, Steve McGuire, Karen Lutz, Carl Lorentz, Marty Smith, Norm Lacasse, and many others whose names I didn't get or forgot to write down. I am particularly grateful to my wife, Barbara, who served as hiking companion, driver, typist, and editor.

Introduction

Hiking is a particular delight to me. Every season there are new things to discover, even on the same old trail. Wildflowers of spring give way to the soft green velvet beauty of summer, which in turn gives way to the color riot of autumn, followed by the snows of winter, with their many animal tracks.

All of us return to the roots of our species when we walk. Our ancestors were bipedal long before they were human. They walked out of the jungle into the veldt and then all over the earth. As an anthropologist would say, bipedalism (walking on two feet) preceded encephalization (swelling of the brain). Our cousins who persisted in walking on their knuckles are still in the Gombe Preserve.

Nessmuck wrote: "We do not go to the woods to rough it, we go to smooth it. We get it rough enough in town." *Nessmuck* is the pen name of George Washington Sears (1821–90), Pennsylvania's pioneer conservationist and outdoor writer.

"Climb the mountains and get their good tidings. Nature's peace will flow into you, and the storms their energy, while cares drop off like autumn leaves," is the way John Muir put it.

According to Thomas Jefferson, "Walking is the best possible exercise. Habituate yourself to walk very far. The Europeans value themselves on having subdued the horse to the uses of man: but I doubt whether we have not lost more than we have gained, by the use of this animal."

And as Aldo Leopold said, "Never did we plan the morrow, for we had learned that in the wilderness some new and irresistible distraction is sure to turn up each day before breakfast."

Hiking in eastern Pennsylvania—despite our region's proximity to the cities along the coast—has much to offer. North Mountain is still wild and remote; the Poconos shelter the most secure portion of the state's bear population; the famous Appalachian Trail follows South and Blue Mountains across Pennsylvania. Saint Anthony's Wilderness, just 20 kilometers north of Harrisburg, is the second largest wild area in the state. Although the state forests are smaller than average, there are many state parks and game lands—some quite large—as well as lands of some public utilities open to the public. A national recreation area and two national historic parks round out the roster. Public lands are limited in extent in eastern Pennsylvania, but well developed with trails.

Trails may traverse woodlands or follow old canals and roads, but many are multiuse, with bicycle and horse as well as foot traffic. On multiuse trails you must pay attention to the rights-of-way of the different trail users. Since horses are easily startled and may throw their riders (sometimes with fatal results), both hikers and bicyclists should give way to horses. Bikers should in turn give way to hikers.

While some trails are heavily used, on others you can still find solitude and a sense of remoteness. There are views,

The author on footlogs

waterfalls, canals, streams, a Civil War battlefield, ghost towns, water gaps, and old railroad grades, as well as quiet paths through the woods and through the largest city park in the world.

GEOGRAPHY

Eastern Pennsylvania contains all the geographic provinces of the state, save one (the Lake Erie Lowlands). These include the Allegheny Plateau and the Ridge and Valley Province. Then, moving from Blue Mountain at the edge of the Ridge and Valley region toward Philadelphia, come the Great Valley; South Mountain and the Reading Prong; the Triassic Lowlands; the Piedmont; and the Coastal Plain.

The Pocono "Mountains" are a southern extension of the Allegheny Plateau, which consists of broad uplands cut by deep, narrow river valleys. The Ridge and Valley Province is made up of wide valleys separated by sharp, narrow ridges. The Allegheny Front forms the boundary between these two regions.

All the other regions lie in the lower right-hand corner of the state. The Great Valley extends from Georgia to New York State; in Pennsylvania it is formed of Cambrian and Ordovician rocks. South Mountain and the Reading Prong are made of Precambrian rocks. The Reading Prong is famous for its radon gas. The Triassic Lowlands were formed when the ancient supercontinent of Pangaea started to break apart about 200 million years ago. The Piedmont is made of a complex of metamorphic rocks of Paleozoic and Precambrian age. The Coastal Plain is of Cretaceous age and cuts across Philadelphia. Look in Van Diver's *Roadside Geology of Pennsylvania* for a map of these different regions.

A large part of eastern Pennsylvania was glaciated during the most recent, or Wisconsin, ice age. The limit of ice advance runs northwest from the Delaware Water Gap, passing through Hickory Run State Park and south of Ricketts Glen State Park. The glacier left scratches on the polished bedrock and great quantities of rocks and silt called glacial till. This debris filled preglacial valleys and forced streams to cut new valleys, with cascades and waterfalls. The glacier also left lakes and swamps—lots of swamps.

SAFETY IN THE WOODS

Once you've parked your car and put a few strong trees between you and the nearest road, the chances of your being injured or killed have dropped by an order of magnitude. Compared with our highways and roads, the woods are relatively safe.

Nevertheless, natural areas may contain hazards not otherwise encountered. Wild animals are seldom a problem. Bears are hunted every year; they know where you are and will ordinarily keep out of your way (if people haven't fed them). Count yourself fortunate if you catch even a glimpse of one. Instead, look for bear sign. Bears protest your use of the trails by leaving piles of scat in the pathway; still, they find using trails easier than crashing through the brush, so they do so. Look for footprints in wet places. They are remarkably human-looking, but wider. You can see all five toes. Look for claw marks at the ends of the toes. (Bears never cut their nails.) Male bears also make scratch marks on trees, particularly evergreens, by clawing off the bark. Watch for large rocks that have been turned over to get at ants underneath, or rotten logs that have been pulled apart for grubs.

Instead of bears, beware of cute little raccoons. Up to 75 percent of raccoons may be rabid, so avoid them all.

Native Americans said of Pennsylvania's animals, "When the pine needle falls from the tree the eagle sees it before it hits the ground, the deer hears the tiny thud, and the bear smells the puff of resin."

What about snakes? There may still be some specimens of timber rattlesnake and copperhead in eastern Pennsylvania. For too many years, though, people have believed that snakes were evil and had to be destroyed. If a snake had a buzzer at one end, then it was a rattlesnake and had to be killed. If it didn't, then it was a copperhead and had to be killed. Snakes have had a hard life in Pennsylvania. Of the 17 or more species of snake in the East, only two are poisonous, the timber rattlesnake and the copperhead. Still, don't pick up any snake: Most snakebites are on the hands or arms rather than the ankles or legs.

Snakes are the easiest wildlife to photograph since they may not flee at your approach. Rattlesnakes and copperheads are your friends, because they live on mice and small rodents. Deer ticks, which carry Lyme disease, spend more time on deer mice than they do on deer. Small rodents eat tree seeds and seedlings; overabundant rodents make it more difficult for the forest to regenerate. As John Muir said, "When we tug at a single thing in nature we find it attached to the rest of the world."

The real threats to your health are microscopic, such as *Giardia* and Lyme disease, or inanimate, such as cold and lightning.

Even the clearest stream or spring must be considered contaminated with *Giardia lamblia* and other harmful bacteria. The *Giardia* organism causes persistent diarrhea. On day hikes you can avoid contaminated water supplies by filling your canteen at home or from some other tested source. For longer trips you will have to purify your drinking water. The easiest way to do so in the field is with a submicron filter. A limitation of such filters is that you must use the cleanest water available or risk clogging the filter while filling a single canteen.

A lighter-weight and cheaper alternative for the patient is to add iodine tablets or drops and wait 20 minutes. A serious limitation is that the water must be at least 20 degrees C (68 degrees F) in order to kill *Giardia* cysts. Many find the iodine taste objectionable. Some submicron filters incorporate an iodine stage. Boiling water to purify it (except in cooking) is recommended only by those who haven't tried it.

Lyme disease is an infection caused by a bacterium that can be transmitted by the bite of some species of ticks. In the eastern United States the *Ixodes,* or deer tick, is the culprit. Deer ticks are smaller than the common dog tick, which does not transmit Lyme disease. The nymph stage, which is responsible for most cases, is smaller than the period at the end of this sentence. The larger adult stage can be seen and removed before it can bite, but you're very unlikely to see the nymph stage. Nor will you feel the bite. Still, if you do discover a tick attached to you, remove it promptly with fine-point tweezers. Grab the tick where the mouthparts enter the skin, and pull gently and repeatedly until the tick lets go by withdrawing its mouthparts. Save the tick in a bottle of alcohol and call your local or state board of health to have it identified.

Ticks are most active in spring and summer—just when you want to go hiking. The conventional wisdom is to wear light-colored (to help you see ticks) long pants and to tuck the pants into your socks, but in warm weather this means you would be courting heat exhaustion instead. Let's face it: In spring, summer, and well into fall, you

Through-hikers on the Appalachian Trail

are going to wear shorts on the trail. What can you do to protect yourself? Spray 20 to 30 percent DEET on your socks and bare legs. (Permanone will keep ticks off your clothes and boots, but should not be applied directly to your skin.) Keep to the middle of the trail; avoid wading through tall grass, brush, or ferns. Don't sit or lie on the ground. As soon as you get home, take a shower to sluice off any unattached ticks.

Blood tests for Lyme disease are still unreliable, so you must be aware of the symptoms and watch out for them. The first symptom is likely to be a slowly expanding red rash that may be centered at the site of the tick bite. The rash may appear from 1 to 4 weeks after the bite. There may be multiple rashes scattered around on parts of your body that are difficult to inspect, such as on your back, under your arms, and behind your knees.

The second symptoms of early Lyme disease are flulike and may include slight fever; headache; swollen glands; fatigue; and stiffness in the joints, neck, and jaw—but no cough or drippy nose. Lyme disease can be treated with antibiotics, and the sooner the better. Untreated Lyme disease can progress to more serious stages involving the joints, heart, and central nervous system, although it is rarely fatal. There is currently no immunization against the disease; a recent vaccine has been withdrawn from the market. Considering the numbers of people at risk, there has been precious little research done on this disease. If you think you may have been exposed, call the American Lyme Disease Foundation at 1-800-876-LYME for the name of a physician in your area who specializes in treating Lyme disease.

For 6 months of the year, whenever the temperature drops below 10 degrees C (50 degrees F), hypothermia stalks the unwary in Penn's Woods. You can forestall it by eating right (don't skip breakfast!), dressing right, and staying dry. Dress in layers so that if you get too hot, you can shed a layer and put it in your pack. (You can get just as wet from your own perspiration as you can from rain or falling into a stream.) Then when you start to feel cold, you can put the layer back on. Don't wait for shivering to start. With hypothermia, your judgment is the first thing to go.

Avoid tall trees and open places during thunderstorms. Along the trail, look for evidence of lightning strikes. A recent strike will appear as a light stripe on the tree and as a long strip of bark, curling across the trail, which blasted off the tree when the sap exploded. A strike from a previous year will have turned dark but will still be visible as a long bare patch running up the tree with a furrow in the middle. If the tree lives long enough, new bark will grow across the scar.

Avoid hiking during bear- and deer-hunting seasons, except on Sundays. New regulations of the Pennsylvania Game Commission require the wearing of safety orange if you hike in game lands during any hunting season, including small game and spring gobbler. An orange cap is a good start, but in addition you need an orange vest or jacket. Wearing of the orange—with apologies to the Irish—is a good idea on *any* public land during the above seasons.

CLOTHING AND EQUIPMENT

The difference between a walker and a hiker is a day pack. A walker must obtain any required supplies along the way. If you are walking in town or at a shopping mall, this is actually possible, but when out in the countryside you had better take your supplies along with you. When you get thirsty, take out your canteen; when you get hungry, take out your lunch; when it starts to rain, take out your poncho; when the insects get annoying, take out your repellent; and when you get turned around, take out your map and compass. If it looks like you're going to spend an unexpected night in the woods (a late start is the easiest way to do this), take out two large plastic garbage bags. Make a hole in the bottom of one bag and put your head through it. Pull the other one up over your legs. You won't sleep much, but you'll be ready to go in the morning. Otherwise the bags will come in handy if you should find trash left by others.

There is a bewildering variety of day packs available on the market, but a good one should be made of nylon and have padded shoulder straps, some outside pockets, and a main compartment. Canvas or even leather would do, but these are heavier than nylon.

Today almost all canteens are plastic, which means that they can be placed in the freezer (allow room for ice to expand) to give you a supply of ice water in summer—although they can't be put on the stove to thaw out in winter. A lunch or snack should contain calories—lots of calories. On the trail, calories are food energy. Lightweight ponchos are made of plastic or coated nylon. A Gore-Tex parka can also provide warmth but will cost more. In winter a sitting pad of 6mm Ensolite is worth its weight. A camera and binoculars are also useful, as is a book of animal tracks. The trouble is to keep the weight of your day pack down to only 4 or 5 kg.

All seasons are hiking seasons. In the warm months you will want to wear shorts and short-sleeved shirts, usually of cotton. The prime requirement is to be comfortable. In cooler weather you will want to switch to long pants and long-sleeved shirts; in cold weather, wool or synthetic pile garments

The trail on Camelback Mountain

and even polypropylene underwear. If the ground is snow-covered, gaiters will close the gap between pants and boots, keeping snow out of your socks. In winter the soft beauty of summer is replaced by a harder aspect, but good country is beautiful year-round.

As Aldo Leopold wrote, "I am glad I shall never be young without wild country to be young in. Of what avail are forty freedoms without a blank spot on the map?"

HIKING BOOTS AND WALKING SHOES

Wet spots, sharp sticks, roots, and rocks grow wild along Pennsylvania's trails. (Hikers have too often been forced back onto those portions of the land that nobody else wants.) So proper footwear is required if you are to avoid unpleasant experiences or even injury. Hiking boots and walking shoes are the most specialized and expensive pieces of a hiker's equipment. Both must have good arch support at the very least.

Hiking boots come in a vast range of prices, and in general you get what you pay for. The cheapest are just glorified sneakers that provide little ankle support. Cheap hiking boots wear out a lot faster than higher-priced ones. Medium-weight leather boots are all you are likely to need on Pennsylvania's trails. The fewer pieces of leather, the better: Most blisters seem to form at seams. Good boots will have lugged soles to give you better footing on the trail, and they will be moderately waterproof.

You may be able to get a lower price on boots by mail order, but good fit is critical. So go to an outdoor store. The clerks there will spoil you for shopping malls because they really know what they are selling. Fit your boots over the socks you will wear on the trail—frequently, a thin inner pair of polypropylene and a thick, mostly wool outer pair.

Walking shoes are low-cut with leather or fabric uppers and some sort of rubber-like sole. They do not provide ankle support and thus are suitable for day hiking on only the best of trails. It doesn't matter whether they are waterproof; since they are low-cut, rain and snow will have plenty of access.

BACKPACKING

Opportunities for backpacking in eastern Pennsylvania are limited to Delaware and Lackawanna State Forests, plus the heavily used Appalachian Trail (AT). The AT is one of the longest trails in the state, but from PA 994 in the west to Totts Gap in the east it is almost entirely on state game lands. The Game Commission has a general ban on camping. Remember that hikers do not contribute to the Game Commission in any way unless they also hunt.

The Game Commission permits shelters along the AT, as well as primitive camping. The rules for primitive camping are given here:

1. Camp within 60 meters of the AT.
2. Camp only 1 night at a given site.
3. Do not camp within 150 meters of a water source or road crossing.
4. No open fires during times of fire danger.

These rules seem quite generous—but the catch is that they apply only to through-hikers. You can hike from A to B, but not back to A. It's true that this rule is rarely enforced, but hikers get upset when it is. Be aware of this limitation if you choose to backpack the AT on game lands.

Trailside shelters concentrate the problems of heavy use. Except in winter, shelters should be avoided on Friday and

Saturday nights. They are likely to be filled, or they may attract local beer parties. You must either stop early or risk finding a shelter already filled beyond capacity.

That said, a good backpack on the AT is between Caledonia and Pine Grove Furnace State Parks. The distance is about 32 kilometers, so it can be done as either a 2- or a 3-day trip. There are shelters at Quarry Gap, Birch Run, and Toms Run; see Potomac Appalachian Trail Club (PATC) map 2–3. As yet no permits are required for backpacking the AT in Pennsylvania.

Backpack camping is permitted in Delaware State Forest along both Thunder Swamp and Blooming Grove Trails. Campsite locations are not designated, but should be at least 15 meters from the trail and at least 100 meters from any road, building, water source, or wetland. A camping permit, still free, is required for all campers. Write to: Delaware State Forest, 474 Clearview Lane, Stroudsbug, PA 18360-3002 or call 570-895-4000. Permits may be faxed if time is short, but applications should ordinarily be made 10 days in advance. All three hikes on the Thunder Swamp Trail plus the Blooming Grove hike could be converted to backpacks.

In Lackawanna State Forest, camping permits, still free, are required for all overnight stays along the Pinchot Trail. Write to Lackawanna State Forest, 401 Samters Building, 101 Penn Avenue, Scranton, PA 18503, or call 570-963-4561. Camping permits can also be obtained at Thornhurst Forest Foreman's Office just east of Thornhurst Picnic Area. Camp at least 15 meters from any trail and 100 meters from any drivable road. Both hikes on the Pinchot Trail could be converted to backpacks.

Be sure to practice minimum-impact camping. A considerable number of books have been written on the techniques of minimal- or zero-impact camping, but the best one is still Harvey Manning's *Backpacking One Step at a Time.* Manning is based in the Pacific Northwest, where the weather is even worse than Pennsylvania's.

ABOUT THIS BOOK

The description of each hike starts with a summary listing the location, the total distance hiked, the time required, the total amount of climbing, highlights along the way, and relevant maps. It should help you decide which hikes match your capabilities and the time available.

Hiking distance has been measured with a Rolatape Model 623m measuring wheel because trail distances are poorly known, except on the AT. Distances are given in kilometers because metrication has become a bottom-up procedure in this country. Metrication is too important to be left to leaders whose commitments are determined by the latest poll.

Hiking times are determined by SOAP/WP (standard old-age pace, with pacemaker). Young hikers will have no trouble shortening them, but bear in mind that hiking is not competitive: It is the quality of the experience that counts. These times do not include lengthy breaks.

Vertical rise is the total amount of climbing on the hike, which may exceed the difference between the highest and lowest points along the way. Vertical rise is determined from U.S. Geological Survey (USGS) topographic maps. Highlights can be lakes, waterfalls, views, ghost towns, ruins, natural areas, or major trails. Maps lists the USGS topographic maps for the hike, plus other maps that may cover the area. Yes, there is a nice map of each hike provided in this book—but if you take a wrong turn, you may stray off the edge of it.

Directions to trailheads are given under "How to Get There," and are still given in miles. Some trailheads are on state routes (*SR*, followed by four digits). These roads are paved, but their quality is one level below that of regular state highways (*PA*, followed by up to three digits). Inconspicuous signs bearing the state route number can be found at the ends of each road and at important junctions along the way. Beware: SR numbers change at county lines in an unpredictable fashion.

Exit numbers on interstates have recently been changed. The old numbers were generally two digits and consecutive: If you passed exit 17, you knew the next exit would be 18 or 16, depending on which way you were going. The new numbers are frequently three digits and merely sequential—but at least they are still integers.

The hikes have been separated into five regions for convenience: South Mountain, bounded by the Mason-Dixon line, Cumberland Valley, and Susquehanna River; Harrisburg and vicinity; Philadelphia and vicinity, bounded by the Mason-Dixon line, Susquehanna and Delaware Rivers, and Blue Mountain; the Poconos, bounded by the Delaware and North Branch of the Susquehanna Rivers, Blue Mountain, and the New York boundary; and North Mountain, bounded by US 220, the New York line, and the North Branch of the Susquehanna River. (I have been generous to the Poconos and included parts of the Ridge and Valley Province with that region, but the Poconos are the best part of eastern Pennsylvania. Besides, the boundaries of the Ridge and Valley region are more complicated to describe.)

I've made every effort to devise circuit hikes, but this has not always been possible. In such cases the hike is described as an in-and-out hike or, if longer, as a car-shuttle hike. Car-shuttle hikes require two cars.

The trips here range from short walks, to half-day hikes (up to 8 km or 3 hours), to all-day hikes, to some real boot-busters (more than 16 km). They cover virtually every type of terrain found in eastern Pennsylvania.

MAPS

State park maps are available from individual park offices or

Bureau of State Parks
P.O. Box 8551
Harrisburg, PA 17105-8551
1-888-PA-PARKS
www.dcnr.state.pa.us

For state game lands (SGL) recreation maps, contact:

Pennsylvania Game Commission
Dept. AR, 2001 Elmerton Avenue
Harrisburg, PA 17110
717-783-7507
www.pgc.state.pa.us

Public-use maps for state forests are available from individual state forest offices or

Bureau of Forestry
Department of Conservation
and Natural Resources
P.O. Box 8552
Harrisburg, PA 17105-8552
717-787-5651
www.dcnr.state.pa.us

For USGS maps:

Distribution Branch
U.S. Geological Survey
Box 25286, Federal Center,
Building 41
Denver, CO 80225
303-202-4700 (five dollars per map)

For PATC maps (write or call for current prices):

Potomac Appalachian Trail Club
118 Park Street, S.E.
Vienna, VA 22180
703-242-0315

TRAIL ORGANIZATIONS

Keystone Trails Association
P.O. Box 129
Confluence, PA 15424-0129
www.kta-hike.org

Membership is still only $15 a year. The four issues per year of the *KTA Newsletter* are alone worth several times the dues. Updates for hikes in this book will be given in the newsletter's "Hiker Alert" column.

Appalachian Trail Conference
P.O. Box 807
Harpers Ferry, WV 25425-0807

BOOKS

Pennsylvania Hiking Trails, 12th edition, 1998. Published by the Keystone Trails Association, P.O. Box 129, Confluence, PA 15424-0129, but available in all the better bookstores. Write for the current price.

Roadside Geology of Pennsylvania, by Bradford B. Van Diver, 1990. Published by Mountain Press Publishing Company. This book will add greatly to your enjoyment of Pennsylvania's exciting geology. A lot happens when continents collide, and you can see much of it from Pennsylvania's trails.

Circuit Hikes in Virginia, West Virginia, Maryland, and Pennsylvania, 5th edition, 1994. Published by the Potomac Appalachian Trail Club, 118 Park Street, S.E., Vienna, VA 22180.

Hiking Pennsylvania, by Rhonda and George Ostertag, 1998. Published by Falcon Publishing Company.

Best Hikes with Children in Pennsylvania, by Sally Trepanowski, 1996. Published by The Mountaineers Books.

Great Hikes in the Poconos and Northeast Pennsylvania, by Boyd and Linda Newman, 2000. Published by Stackpole Books.

Hike Pennsylvania, by John Young, 2001. Published by The Globe Pequot Press.

Natural Pennsylvania, by Charles Fergus, 2002. Published by Stackpole Books.

Hiking the Endless Mountains, by Jeff Mitchell, 2003. Published by Stackpole Books.

Gettysburg Heritage Trail Guide, 9th edition, by Costa Dillon and William Curtis, 1993. Published by Boy Scouts of America York-Adams Council.

South Mountain

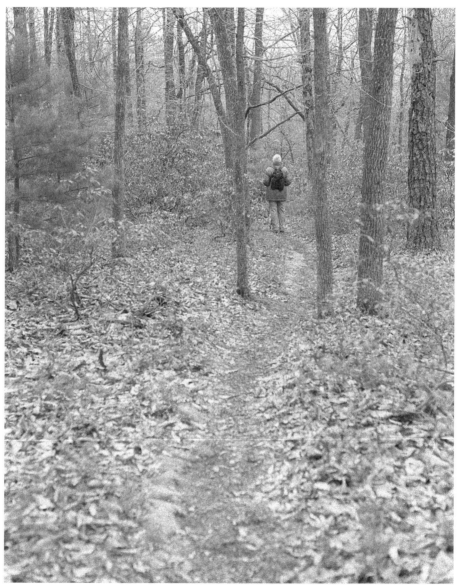

A hiker on the trail at Rocky Knob

1

Caledonia State Park

Location: 9 miles east of Chambersburg

Distance: 4.7 km (2.9 miles)

Time: 1 3/4 hours

Vertical rise: 175 meters (575 feet)

Highlights: Relics of the charcoal iron era

Maps: USGS 71/2' Caledonia Park; PATC map 2–3; park map

Caledonia Park was first opened as an amusement park by a trolley company, much as Pen Mar on the Maryland border was operated. Caledonia is named for a charcoal iron furnace operated by Thaddeus Stevens— abolitionist, statesman, and father of the public school system in Pennsylvania. The iron furnace operated from 1837 to a few days before the Battle of Gettysburg, in 1863, when it was destroyed by Confederate troops under Jubal Early.

In addition to the Appalachian Trail, there are 15 km of trails in the park. This circuit hike uses two trails in the eastern part of the park and adjacent lands of Michaux State Forest. These trails follow old charcoal roads and the millrace and, except for a short section between them, are relatively free of rocks, so walking shoes should be adequate.

How to Get There

Caledonia State Park is located at the junction of US 30 with PA 233 between Chambersburg and Gettysburg. This junction is 8.8 miles east of exit 16 off I-81, on US 30. You can park at the Iron Furnace Monument lot on PA 233 just north of US 30.

The Trail

Start your hike just to the left of the half-scale replica of the furnace stack on the Thaddeus Stevens Trail. Pass a junction with the Charcoal Hearth Trail, on which you will return, and cross a bridge over the mill-race. The iron furnace was of the "cold blast" type, which required a waterwheel to

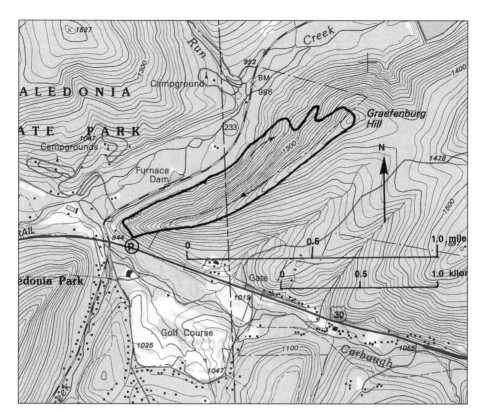

operate the bellows. If the blast failed for any reason—which happened all too often—the furnace would cool off and its contents solidify. Then the entire stack would have to be rebuilt.

Cross the millrace, which still carries water, and continue along it. There are occasional yellow paint blazes. PA 233 is just to your left. Recross the millrace and continue on the Charcoal Hearth Trail, which is rough at first. Furnace Dam, which furnishes water to the millrace, is on the far side of PA 233. Next, pass the organized group camp and, at 1.4 km, bear right on a charcoal road that climbs Piney Mountain and draws away from PA 233.

A charcoal iron furnace required the charcoal from a hectare of forest every day it ran. Trees were cut, stripped of bark, and

stacked on a flat piece of ground dug out of the mountainside. The pile was then covered over with leaves, earth, and sod—to limit the airflow—and set on fire. Producing charcoal took anywhere from 1 to 4 weeks. The process required continuous attention, as the fire could either go out if it got too little air or turn the pile to worthless ash if it got too much. After cooling, the charcoal was transported by wagons along the charcoal roads, which were also built by hand.

First you will reach hearth 5, followed by hearth 4. Hearth 3 is on a side trail to your left. Then pass hearths 2 and 1. All are marked with signs. At 2.6 km you arrive at the 465-meter summit of Graefenburg Hill, marked by a post in the ground. Soon you encounter white blazes marking the bound-

Millrace

ary between Michaux State Forest and the park. This is a delightful ridgetop trail. Your path descends slowly, and the noise from US 30 becomes louder. Turn left onto the Thaddeus Stevens Trail at the bridge over the millrace and follow it back to your car.

Additional hiking at Caledonia can be found on the Ramble Trail, a short loop on both sides of Conococheague Creek in the western side of the park. Other loops are possible; see Hike 22 in *Circuit Hikes in Virginia, West Virginia, Maryland, and Pennsylvania.*

2

Rocky Knob

Location: 7 miles north of Caledonia State Park on US 30

Distance: 6.9 km (4.3 miles)

Time: 2½ hours

Vertical rise: 165 meters (550 feet)

Highlights: View, designated hiking trail

Maps: USGS 7½' Caledonia Park, PATC map 2–3, trail brochure

This is a short loop hike in Michaux State Forest. Rocky Knob Trail is the only designated hiking trail in this forest district. (Of course the Appalachian Trail—which you'll cross on this hike—is protected from horses, bikes, and ATVs by both federal and state legislation.) A lengthy multiuse trail in Michaux provides plenty of opportunity for horses and bikes. In addition there is an ATV trail in Michaux, which has provided helpful statistics about ATV usage. More than 55 percent of the riders violate regulations on this trail, showing that the bad name accorded ATVs is not due to just a few "bad apples."

Rocky Knob Trail was built in 1976 by the Youth Conservation Corps (YCC), a job training program of the time. The trail incorporates a road started by the Civilian Conservation Corps (CCC) in 1937. The CCC was probably the most successful of all Franklin Roosevelt's New Deal programs, but the rocks here proved too much for it; the CCC was unable to complete this road all the way to Birch Run Road.

How to Get There

To reach Rocky Knob Trail from the south, proceed north on PA 233 from the traffic light on US 30 in Caledonia State Park. After 1.6 miles, turn left onto the unpaved Milesburn Road and continue for 4.1 miles to its junction with Ridge Road. Turn right and follow Ridge Road for 1.5 miles, crossing the Appalachian Trail (AT) along the way. There is parking on the left side of the road, but the low-profile sign is behind the gate

The map labels

To PA 233

Gate 1512

Gates

1800

1700

1900

Ridge Road

P 1873

APPALACHIAN

B I G

1700

Sier Hill
× 1938

1900

Knob

1644

Rocky Knob
× 1882

Hill

1800

F L A T

A T

NATIONAL

R I D G E

SCENIC

1917

× 1986

Shelter

TRAIL

1800

1900

1800

1716 Gate

Gate

BR 1638

1900

× 1982

F L A T

Strasbau
Hill

G

Run

1600

BR 1505

× 1605

Ditch

S T

2. Rocky Knob

Appalachian Trail

P Parking

N

View

0   1/2 mile

0   1/2 kilometer

---

on the right. From the north, turn right off PA 233 onto the paved Shippensburg Road and climb to Big Flat, crossing the AT. After 2.4 miles, turn left onto Ridge Road and proceed 2.1 miles to the small parking area.

The Trail

To start your hike, pass the gate and follow the orange blazes along the narrow old road. The Rocky Knob Trail was originally blazed green, and you will see that the re-blazing has not been perfect. At 250 meters you cross the white-blazed AT. If you should wish to extend your hike, Caledonia Park and Georgia are to the right; Pine Grove Furnace Park and Maine are to the left.

Trees growing along the trail are black gum, pitch pine, and chestnut oak, while the ground cover is mostly mountain laurel and scrub oak. Sassafras is also found here.

The woolly adelgid, an aphid, produces whitish masses on hemlock needles

These plants are indicators of some of the poorest soils in the state. The soils on South Mountain are derived from sandstones and are rocky and sandy with little organic material. Forest fires over the years may have destroyed the humus.

At 700 meters turn left on trail at post 1. Various points of interest along the trail are marked with these numbered posts. Many of these points involve living things, such as Allegheny mound ants and American chestnuts. These items have a habit of moving on, leaving the post to puzzle hikers, but some of these posts have been moved in an effort to catch up. You'll have little doubt if you find an active colony of Allegheny mound ants: The hill may be 5 meters in diameter and more than a meter high. Keep moving past the mound, as the ants are quite aggressive and can inflict painful bites.

At post 6 there is a leaves-off view across Birch Run to a spur of Big Flat Ridge. A cleared view of Rocky Knob and Long Pine Reservoir at 2.3 km is marked by post 9. Big Flat Ridge and Piney Mountain are visible beyond.

Look for coyote scat in the trail. If it is very fresh, the coyote may be moving along the trail in front of you just out of sight; the animal uses this means to register its displeasure at being disturbed. Older scat will be full of fur, and last year's will show a core of pulverized bone. Coyotes are almost exclusively carnivorous.

Up to this point the trail has been fairly flat, but it now descends steeply to a col between Sier Hill and Rocky Knob itself. Rocky Knob is a boulder pile composed of quartzite. Quartzite is the metamorphic form of sandstone—the individual grains have been fused together.

Look for American chestnut sprouts along the trail. The leaves are bladelike and serrated. Early in the 20th century every other tree from Maine to Georgia was an American chestnut. The ideal forest species, it provided food for people and wildlife, a cash crop in Appalachia. Its rot-resistant wood could be used for everything from fence posts to picture frames. And it didn't have to be replanted: It resprouted from stumps. Then came the chestnut blight, an imported fungus. The American chestnut was reduced to occasional shoots that spout from underground stumps, the only part of the tree resistant to the blight. A hybrid chestnut is being developed and should be available for planting in a few years.

At 3.8 km avoid an old trail to your left and continue to descend, entering a stand of white pines and hemlocks. The hemlocks are infested by the woolly adelgid, another imported pest. Within a few years our state tree may follow the American chestnut into oblivion.

It doesn't always take an asteroid to produce a mass extinction.

Turn right onto the old CCC road at 3.9 km and start the gentle climb back to the top of South Mountain. An unmarked, unmaintained trail at this junction leads downhill to Birch Run Road. The quartzites below this point proved too much for the CCC crew back in 1937. Post 14 at 4.2 km marks a spring—nice and cold, but use your water filter before you drink it. Without a filter, stick to your canteen. You can hear the run to your left, but you have no chance to see it before you near the top of the hollow. By then it is just a trickle.

At 6.2 km pass post 1, completing the loop, and continue ahead to return to your car.

3

Pole Steeple

Location: 8 miles south of exit 37 off I-81

Distance: 8.7 km (5.4 miles)

Time: 3¼ hours

Vertical rise: 232 meters (760 feet)

Highlights: View, Appalachian Trail

Maps: USGS 7½' Dickinson; PATC map 2–3; park map

The famous Appalachian Trail (AT) passes through Pine Grove Furnace State Park on its way from Springer Mountain in Georgia to Mount Katahdin in Maine. The halfway point is just east of the park. In-season, look for through-hikers along this trail. They tend to be lean and have neat but worn-looking backpacks. If the temperature is much above freezing, they will be wearing shorts. Northbounders pass through Pine Grove Furnace in June, while southbounders don't get here until September.

This circuit hike uses the white-blazed Appalachian Trail, a blue-blazed side trail, and a dead-end but paved road. It visits a natural overlook above Laurel Lake called Pole Steeple. This quartzite cliff was named by Boy Scouts who planted a flagpole on top of it. The name persists, but the pole is long gone.

Pine Grove Furnace was a charcoal iron furnace that operated from 1837 to 1863. Operation of the ore pit that is now Fuller Lake continued until 1893, when the pit flooded. At most state park swimming areas the certain drowning depth is just above the knee, but at Fuller Lake the swimming area is 13 meters deep!

You will want your boots for this hike, as the AT footway is rocky and the descent through the cliffs at Pole Steeple is very rocky.

How to Get There

Pine Grove Furnace State Park is located on PA 233, 8.1 miles south of exit 37 off I-81 (between Carlisle and Shippensburg) and 13.5 miles northeast of US 30 at Caledonia. Proceed east on Hunters Run

Road for 0.2 mile, then turn south into the Fuller Lake parking lot.

The Trail

Start your hike at the far corner of the parking lot. Immediately after passing the dressing stockade for the beach, turn left onto a gravel path. The white blazes proclaim that this is part of the AT. At the corner of a meadow is a confusing double blaze. Ignore it and continue on the gravel path past the food concession. Then cross bridges over Mountain Creek and the outlet from Fuller Lake.

Continue on a wide trail along Mountain Creek. This is the route of the South Mountain Railroad, which served the ironworks. This part of the AT is also open to bicycles.

At 0.8 km you pass the Swamp Trail, a loop trail to your right. Mountain Creek is on your left.

Turn right at 1.2 km and begin to climb Piney Mountain along the white blazes of the AT. Bicycles are not permitted beyond this point. Maine is ahead of you and Georgia, behind. Soon you cross a meadow and reach the halfway point of the AT. Every time the AT is relocated, this point shifts north or south. Originally it was at Center Point Knob, a good day's hike north of here. About 80 percent of AT relocations are longer than the original trail.

Shortly after you reach the top of Piney Mountain, a couple of charcoal hearths are to your left. During the charcoal iron days, the entire South Mountain area was clearcut repeatedly on a 20- to 25-year cycle to feed the iron furnaces. Next, pass an unblazed trail from your right.

Turn left onto the blue-blazed Old Forge Road (not drivable) at 3.5 km. Continue past two unmarked trails to your left. Turn left on trail at 3.8 km and climb steeply to Pole Steeple, which turns out to be a quartzite cliff. Be careful, as there is quite an adequate drop to the rocks below. Before you is Laurel Lake, formed by a dam on Mountain Creek. Beyond is the main body of South Mountain.

The cliffs at Pole Steeple

If you're afraid of heights, the best course would be to retrace your steps to the park. To continue the circuit, though, bear left to the spot where the blue blazes descend very steeply through a break in the cliffs. This break is actually a 300-million-year-old fault. The rocks moved along this zone as continents collided, and you can see the resulting polished surfaces called slickensides.

After entering the woods at the bottom of the cliffs, you pass several more charcoal hearths. Turn left onto paved Railroad Road along the shore of Laurel Lake at 5.1 km. Mountain Creek is visible at several places. Along the way you pass the Ice House Trail, which crosses Mountain Creek, and at 7.5 km you close the loop. Continue ahead on the former railroad grade, now the AT, to return to your car.

Additional hiking opportunities at Pine Grove Furnace include Sunset Rocks (Hike 8).

4

Kings Gap

Location: 5 miles southeast of exit 37 off I-81

Distance: 10.1 km (6.3 miles)

Time: 3¾ hours

Vertical rise: 340 meters (1,115 feet)

Highlights: Mountain stream, views

Maps: USGS 7½' Dickinson; park map

Kings Gap Environmental Education Center is located on the north edge of South Mountain in Cumberland County. Unlike a regular state park, this park's primary mission is education. Busloads of schoolchildren come to learn about the out-of-doors and Pennsylvania's natural heritage. I'm sure that any break from classroom routine seems like fun, and the children are unaware of the painless education going on.

Starting in 1906, James Cameron, grandson of Simon Cameron—who served in the U.S. Senate and as secretary of war to President Lincoln—began buying land here. The tract eventually reached 1,100 hectares. He built the 32-room mansion at the top of the hill. Its architecture might be termed "bunker"—the house was furnished in haute hunting camp—but the view from its terrace across Cumberland Valley is unmatched. What a place to be lord of all you survey! James Cameron introduced conservation measures to restore the land, which had been abused by a century and a half of charcoal production for the local iron furnaces. Along this hike you can see how successful these efforts have been.

After Cameron's death in 1949, 580 hectares, including the 32-room "cottage," were purchased by Masland and Son Carpet Company of Carlisle, which used the mansion as a guest house. In 1973, with the aid of The Nature Conservancy, the Masland tract was acquired for the state.

You will want your boots for this hike, due to the rocks and wet places along Kings Gap Hollow Run.

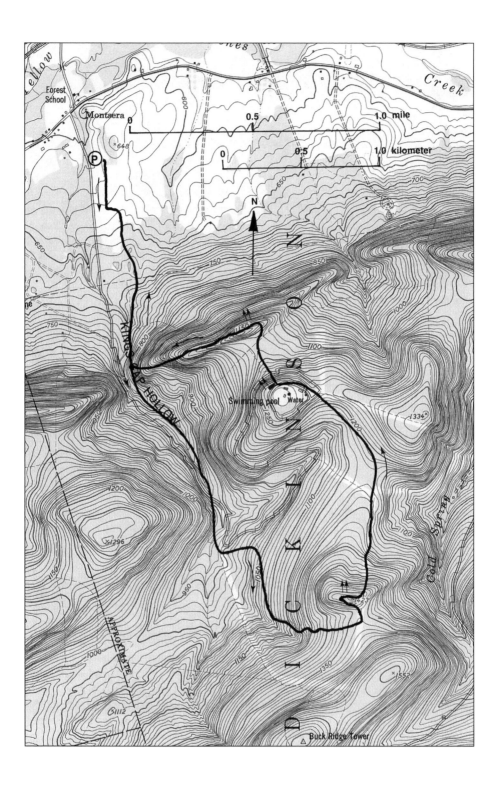

How to Get There

Kings Gap can be reached from exit 37 off I-81. Drive south on PA 233 for 2.5 miles, then east on SR 3006 for 2.3 miles. Turn south onto Kings Gap Hollow Road. Kings Gap can also be reached from PA 34 just north of Mount Holly Springs. Drive west on SR 3006 for 4.5 miles; then turn south.

On Kings Gap Hollow Road it is only 0.2 mile to the Pine Plantation Day-Use Area. Turn left to the parking lot. Thirty thousand pines were planted in this 17-hectare plot back in the 1950s. Pick up a copy of the trail map of Kings Gap, usually available at the display map.

The Trail

Make your way left behind the solar composting toilet, following the paved trail for handicapped access. Soon you come to a restored log cabin in a clearing. Leave the paved trail and pick up the red-blazed Rock Scree Trail, which follows a woods road straight through the plantation of Douglas fir, larch, and white pine—lots of white pine. The pine plantation is being thinned to permit continued growth.

Cross the Pine Plantation Trail; turn left between a vernal pond to your right and a stone wall to your left. Turn right and cross an unblazed trail. Climb past a charcoal hearth and, at 1.7 km, turn right onto the blue-blazed Ridge Overlook Trail. Descend and turn left onto the yellow-blazed Kings Gap Hollow Trail along the stream. Proceed upstream to a crossing of paved Kings Gap Hollow Road. Follow the Watershed Trail ahead, over a bridge and past a small pond. Continue through a stand of young white pines and bear left to a parking area. (The map says the Watershed Trail is blazed purple, but the blazes looked white to me.) Pass an open-air classroom and reach the parking lot at 3.3 km.

Cross the parking lot and pick up the orange-blazed Scenic Vista Trail. This trail was built and is maintained by the Susquehanna Appalachian Trail Club. The Scenic Vista Trail follows charcoal roads to 4.6 km, where you turn left on trail. After a climb you reach a view north over the Cumberland Valley. A stand of pitch pines frames the vista. Beyond, the trail descends through the woods, crossing an old swath and turning left to reach a power line. Turn left to a parking area on the paved road at 6.8 km.

The Scenic Vista Trail continues below the mansion (which is open to the public) to a junction with the Rock Scree Trail. To see the attractive view from the terrace, continue ahead on the Rock Scree Trail and then turn left up an unmarked path to the terrace. This view extends from Blue Mountain Tunnel in the west to Wagoners Gap in the east. Retrace your steps and continue down the Rock Scree Trail, crossing the paved road for the last time.

Next, cross the Forest Heritage Trail twice and continue on the Ridge Overlook Trail. The Rock Scree Trail diverges to your left; if the ridge is socked in with fog, you might want to stay on Rock Scree instead. At 7.8 km you reach a last view over the Cumberland Valley. Turn right onto the Rock Scree Trail at 8.5 km and retrace your steps to your car.

This hike uses only 4 of the 12 trails at Kings Gap. Additional loops can be made on the Boundary and Watershed Trails, and on the Maple Hollow and Forest Heritage Trails—among others.

5

York Heritage Trail

Location: *Between I-83 and PA 616*

Distance: *10.3 km (6.4 miles)*

Time: *3 hours*

Vertical rise: *None*

Highlights: *Tunnel, stream*

Maps: *USGS 7½' York, West York, Glen Rock, Seven Valleys; park map*

Eastern Pennsylvania has many rail-trails, but this one comes well recommended—and it is certainly heavily used. It follows the grade of the Northern Central Railroad, once a vital link from Washington, D.C., to Lake Ontario and upstate New York. In 1863 the Confederate troops of Robert E. Lee destroyed bridges and cut telegraph wires here prior to the Battle of Gettysburg in their efforts to isolate Washington from the rest of the country.

The trail is operated by the York County Department of Parks and Recreation but lies adjacent to an active railroad. Stay clear of the tracks at all times, and cross only at established crossings. The tracks are rusty and there do not appear to be any signals along the track, so trains must be infrequent; still, excursion trails remain a definite possibility. Horseback riders are implored in boldface type on the park map to clean up after their horses, but this request appears to be honored only in the breach. This is a car-shuttle hike.

How to Get There

From exit 14 off I-83 south of York, take PA 182 west for 2.6 miles and turn left onto Croll School Road (SR 3042). After another 0.5 mile, turn right onto Days Mill Road. The parking lot for Brillhart station is on your left just beyond the tracks. Leave one car here. The station building is long gone. In your other car, turn left onto Days Mill Road. After 1.8 mile bear left onto Indian Rock Dam Road, and at 2.2 miles turn left onto PA 616 at a traffic light. At 5.6

5. York Heritage Trail
Ⓟ Parking
N
0   1/2 mile
0   1/2 kilometer

A light at the end of the tunnel

miles and the junction with PA 214, make sure you are still on south PA 616. Turn left at 6.6 miles into the parking lot at Hanover Junction. This station has been restored to its appearance in 1863 when Abe Lincoln changed trains here on his way to deliver the Gettysburg Address. It contains a small museum open on Saturdays. Drinking water and rest rooms are available. Only the stations at Hanover Junction and New Freedom still exist. Others such as Brillhart survive in name only.

The Trail

Cross the tracks and turn left onto the crushed-stone path. Cross a bridge over the south branch of Codorus Creek but stay on the trail as it passes through private farmlands. The banks are adorned with Virginia creeper, multiflora rose, poison ivy, and NO TRESPASSING signs. The trail is equipped with benches, picnic tables, and mileposts. Walnut, pin oak, chokecherry, sassafras, and hickory grow along the right-of-way.

At 1.3 km you cross a viaduct over PA 214 (Main Street) in the village of Seven Valleys. Just beyond is the Seven Valleys access area. PA 214 continues, paralleling the trail to your right. Old railroad mileposts have been left along the trail. Cross to the other side of the tracks at 3.4 km. Just beyond, you cross a bridge over Codorus Creek, and at 3.9 km you cross over the tracks again. A steel road bridge sits in a field to your left; to your right you can see where it once crossed Codorus Creek. If the bridge is judged to be historic, it cannot be dismantled but must wait until a good home is found for it. At 4.5 km you cross the tracks again, also crossing Glatfelters Station Road. At 5.8 km the route becomes generally wooded. Note that adjacent lands are protected from development by the Farm and Natural Lands Trust of York County.

Beyond, the railroad grade is cut into the side of a hill. Picnic tables along this section are covered. Beyond the 15-mile post you can see Howard Tunnel ahead. Not to worry if you forgot your flashlight: The tunnel is only 78 meters long, and you can see right through it. Why didn't Confederate raiders collapse the tunnel before the Battle of Gettysburg?

At 8.1 km you'll reach a bridge over a road and stream, followed by a road crossing at grade. Cross the tracks again at 8.6 km. At 10.3 km turn left onto Days Mill Road to the Brillhart station parking lot.

For additional hiking opportunities on York Heritage Trail, you can continue another 6 or 7 km to its north end in York; south of Hanover Junction, it runs nearly 18 km to the Mason-Dixon line.

6

Gifford Pinchot State Park

Location: 10 miles south of Harrisburg

Distance: 11.1 km (6.9 miles)

Time: 3½ hours

Vertical rise: 80 meters (260 feet)

Highlights: Mason-Dixon Trail

Maps: USGS 7½' Wellsville, Dover; park map; Mason-Dixon Trail System map 2

Gifford Pinchot was a two-term governor of Pennsylvania. Appointed to be the first forester of the United States by President Theodore Roosevelt, he helped designate 200 million acres of public lands as national forest. He is regarded as one of the prime movers in the conservation movement. In Pennsylvania, Pinchot is regarded as a hero of conservation. There is even a chapter of the Sierra Club named for him. But in California Pinchot is remembered as a villain, because he permitted the damming of Hetch Hetchy, the second Yosemite Valley. The fight to save Hetch Hetchy was led by John Muir himself, and the failure to protect this valley led directly to the formation of the Sierra Club, still one of the strongest conservation groups in the country.

As governor of Pennsylvania, Pinchot fostered a program to pave rural roads and "get the farmer out of the mud." "Pinchot Roads," as they were called, were hard-surfaced and high-crowned. The first such road is now PA 177, which now forms the northwest boundary of Gifford Pinchot State Park.

The Mason-Dixon Trail starts at the Brandywine Trail in Chadds Ford and heads south through Delaware and Maryland before heading north along the Susquehanna River. It meets the Appalachian Trail at Whiskey Springs on South Mountain. There is little public land along it, and most of its route follows low-use public roads. One of the longest off-road sections is here in Gifford Pinchot State Park. It strings together several shorter trails, which you'll walk on this hike, as it passes through the park.

How to Get There

This is a car-shuttle hike. You can reach Gifford Pinchot Park from exit 35 off I-83; follow the signs for PA 177 south. It is 5.9 miles to the park. Turn left onto Alpine Road and proceed 0.5 mile to the dam. The Lake Side Trail emerges here. There is room for two or three cars to park here, but do not block the gate. If more space is needed, park at the overlook picnic area and add 200 meters on Alpine Road to your hike. Leave one car here.

Return to PA 177. Turn left and drive 3.5 miles to the traffic light in Rossville. Turn right onto PA 74. In just 0.3 mile turn right onto Squire Gratz Road and go 0.6 mile to the Beaver Creek Trail and parking area.

You can also reach the park from York by heading northwest on PA 74; and from Dillsburg (along US 15) by heading southeast on PA 74.

The Trail

Head into the woods on the Beaver Creek Trail, following the blue blazes. Turns are indicated by double blazes in which the upper blaze is displaced in the direction of the turn. The trail passes eastern red cedar, white oak, white pine, and shagbark hickory trees to reach the bank of Beaver Creek. At

Mason-Dixon Trail

times you see old stone walls in the forest; these walls border fields that are now reverting to woods.

At 1.4 km you pass some ledges to your right and then more white pines. These are followed by a short section of puncheon and a footbridge over an inlet. You reach boat-mooring area 1, with rest rooms, and cross PA 177 (use caution) at 2.5 km. Continue on the Mockingbird Trail, which leads to the shore of Pinchot Lake and then inland. There is plenty of poison ivy here.

Cross under a pole line at 3.3 km and continue along the park boundary. Traverse a stream as best you can at 4.0 km, and reach a paved road at 4.6 km. The contact station for the campground is visible to your left. Continue through the woods on a relocation that gets the trail off East Camp Area Road.

Turn left onto the Ridge Trail at 5.6 km; continue past a junction with the Old Farm Trail to your left. Next you reach the Pinchot Trail. These junctions are marked with routed post signs.

At 7.1 km, turn left on paved road to the Conewago Day-Use Area. Pass a ball field to your right, then turn right past pavilion 1. Turn right onto the Alpine Trail, and right again onto an old woods road. Reach a junction with the Midland Trail at 8.1 km; continue ahead on Midland, crossing a footbridge, followed by the big climb of the day. Stay on the Midland Trail where the Fern Trail goes off to your right. Tulip trees grow along this section.

At 8.5 km turn right onto the Lake Side Trail North, and right again at the edge of the lake. Then pass a particularly well-built old stone wall to reach another junction with the Fern Trail. Cross boat-mooring area 3 and jog right at a couple of picnic tables under a large spruce tree.

The trail continues along the lake; large boulders afford views across the water. At 11.8 km you reach the corner of the dam that forms Pinchot Lake. Proceed to Alpine Road and your car.

For additional hiking opportunities at Gifford Pinchot, you could explore a network of trails near the campground or a loop formed by the Quaker Race Trail and Lake Side Trail on the other side of the lake.

7

Gettysburg

Location: On US 15, about 5 miles north of the Mason-Dixon line

Distance: 13.0 km (8.1 miles)

Time: 5½ hours

Vertical rise: 140 meters (460 feet)

Highlights: Little Round Top, Pickett's Charge

Maps: USGS 7½' Gettysburg, Fairfield

You've seen the TV series and the movie. Enough of virtual reality. On this hike, with just a tad of imagination you can experience Gettysburg on your own as you reenact Pickett's Charge or the defense of Little Round Top.

You might think there wouldn't be an opportunity for hiking at a national military park, but that's not the case. Although in the 1860s soldiers were sometimes carried on trains or boats or rode horseback, they mostly moved and fought on foot. You can get a much better idea of what they faced if you are on foot rather than in a car.

This hike is based on the Billy Yank Trail in the *Gettysburg Heritage Trail Guide,* published by the Boy Scouts of America. The *Billy Yank* name is not entirely accurate, as the route takes you along both sides of the battle line. The route visits Little Round Top and the site of Pickett's Charge, places where decisive actions took place on the second and third days of the Battle of Gettysburg. Despite the monuments and markers that pepper the landscape, it is still possible to feel something of what the two armies experienced here for three days in July 1863.

The battle resulted from Lee's invasion of the North in June following his triumph at Chancellorsville. He planned to threaten Harrisburg and Philadelphia in order to draw the Union army into the field; he would then destroy it in a defensive battle. The threat to these cities was blunted when the bridge over the Susquehanna River at Columbia was burned by the local militia.

While Lee's troops were foraging for supplies, they collided with Union troops near the town of Gettysburg. (With 10 or 11 roads, Gettysburg was the road hub of southern Pennsylvania.) Along the way the Confederates burned Thaddeus Stevens's iron furnace at Caledonia (see Hike 1).

By July 2 the two armies were on parallel ridges south of Gettysburg. As you will see, these ridges are so low as to be barely discernible except at Big and Little Round Tops. (Lee's forces had carried the day on July 1, breaking the Union line north of town and driving the Federals back to the low hills south of town. Along this hike you will see what happened on July 2 and 3.)

There are a couple of drinking fountains along the way, but make sure you have your canteen, and a hat. You will need good walking shoes or boots. There are some rocks and a lot of horse-trodden mud on this hike.

How to Get There

The trailhead is the terrace on the west side of the Cyclorama Center. To reach it, drive north on Tanneytown Road (PA 134) from US 15 for 2.9 miles, following signs to the visitors center. It can also be reached from the town of Gettysburg; it's about 1 mile south of the town center.

Park at the Cyclorama lot, if possible, or the visitors center lot. Stop in at the center to get a pamphlet for the Round Top Trail, a park map and loop trail sheet (free), and the *Heritage Trail Guide* in the bookstore.

The Trail

To start, make your way to the west side of the Cyclorama Center, then head south along the paved High Water Mark Trail. At 100 meters bear right and continue south along Hancock Avenue. Look out for traffic. Note that the avenues were not here at the time of the battle; roads and pikes were here instead. The Angle—an offset in the stone wall—is to your right. You will return there late in the hike.

At 500 meters the paved High Water Mark Trail ends. Continue south toward the Pennsylvania monument. It is the largest one you will see. What would these monuments and memorials look like if Maya Lin had designed them?

Note the Tammany monument: It's the one with the tepee and a Native American wearing feathers. Some Native American units did fight for the Confederacy, west of the Mississippi. Pass the Pennsylvania monument and continue to the Minnesota monument: It's the one with a soldier running with a rifle. The lst Minnesota suffered 65 percent casualties in the battle.

Turn right at the Minnesota monument and proceed across a field to a post-and-rail fence. Then turn left and follow the fence to United States Avenue. Turn right and pass General Sickles's headquarters. On July 2 Sickles advanced his Union corps beyond Cemetery Ridge, defying orders, inviting attack, and leaving Little Round Top undefended. The attack wasn't long in coming.

Now turn left onto Sickles Avenue, and left again onto Wheatfield Road. Continue on this road to a metal sign that says WHEAT-FIELD. Turn left across the Wheatfield. Two hours of fighting on July 2 left the field covered with bodies without giving either side an advantage.

When you hit a paved road (Sickles Avenue again), turn right and then left on De Trobriand Avenue. Follow De Trobriand past the monument for the 110th Pennsylvania to a metal sign that says DE TROBRIAND AVENUE. Turn left here and follow an old railroad grade. This was the bed of a trolley line built to bring an earlier generation of visitors to Devil's Den and Little Round Top. There

are two footbridges along this section. Cross Brooke Avenue. The trolley grade comes to an end, but you continue across a footbridge over Plum (or Bloody) Run. At 5.2 km you reach a drinking fountain. Rest rooms are to your right and Devil's Den, to your left.

Avoid a road to your right and continue straight ahead to Warren Avenue. Turn right and then pick a path up Little Round Top. From up here you get an idea of its strategic importance, which was realized late on July 2 by Brigadier General Warren (his statue overlooks Devil's Den). The Confederate attackers were beaten back, but just barely.

Beyond the top, make your way to the parking lot and turn right. After 150 meters bear left on a paved path to the monument for the 20th Maine. Under the command of Joshua Lawrence Chamberlain, the 20th Maine repulsed a series of assaults that would have flanked Little Round Top. With ammunition exhausted, Chamberlain ordered a bayonet charge that routed the Rebel attackers. Lee had come within a whisker of winning the second day at Gettysburg.

To continue your hike, follow the path down to a small parking lot on Wright Avenue. Turn left onto Wright and, after 40 meters, turn right onto a horse trail. This leads up the slope of Big Round Top to a junction with the Loop Trail. Bear left on the Loop Trail, which is fitted with posts as a nature trail. (These posts can be interpreted with the sheet you picked up at the visitors center.) Big Round Top, although higher than Little Round Top, did not have the same strategic importance because it was wooded, then as now. Little Round Top had been cleared a few months before the battle.

Bear right on the Loop Trail at the next junction. At post 14 turn left, then left again

onto South Confederate Avenue. After 55 meters turn right onto a path next to a split-rail fence. This takes you to Granite Farm and the end of a gravel road. Follow the gravel road to the junction of Confederate Avenue and Emmittsburg Road. Cross with care.

Turn right along West Confederate Avenue and follow it along the Confederate front line on Warfield Ridge, going by the Arkansas monument.

Pass the observation tower, then cross Millerstown Road. Continue north on West Confederate Avenue. After Pitzer Woods, turn left into the amphitheater parking lot. In-season there are drinking fountains here.

Keep left of the amphitheater and follow the horse trail through the woods. When the horse trail nears West Confederate Avenue again, look through the trees for the Virginia memorial topped with General Lee riding Traveler. Follow a path out to the avenue and pass by the memorial. This was the starting point of Pickett's Charge on July 3. It is 1.4 km to the Angle—and all in the open.

Fifteen thousand Confederates emerge from the trees and start across the fields. Their aiming point is that grove of trees you can see on Cemetery Ridge. They are faced by 9,000 Federals.

Conventional military wisdom says the attacking force should have numbered at least 27,000. Why did Lee make such a mistake and depart from his game plan? As novelist and Civil War historian Shelby Foote has said, Lee's blood was up by this time. He had won the first day and had come so close on the second. His supplies were running low. One more attack could change the course of the war: Recognition of the Confederacy by England and France might follow.

Pickett's Charge was preceded by a 2-hour artillery duel. A German military observer called it a waste of powder. Follow

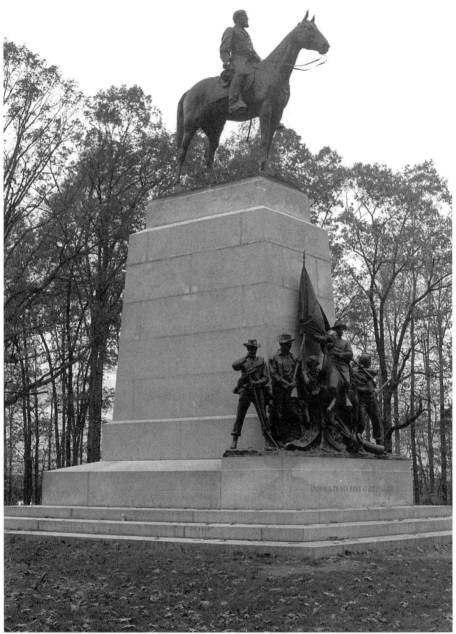

General Robert E. Lee

the route of General Pickett's men toward the far rise. Imagine that 9,000 men are shooting at you.

At first the fire is cannons with explosive and solid shot. But as you approach, musket fire is added and the cannons switch to canister. Canister turns a cannon into a giant shotgun. With each shot, great gaps are torn in the advancing formation. A few men make it to the Federal line at the Angle. But there are not enough of them. They are killed or captured. The survivors stream back toward Seminary Ridge. Lee rides out to meet them. "My fault, my fault," he is saying.

General Meade's failure to counterattack or even pursue the Confederates led to the perception that Gettysburg had been a Confederate victory. Vicksburg surrendered to Union forces on July 4, and it was thought that the South had broken even. Only later did it slowly become apparent that Gettysburg was not a victory for the South.

Nor was it a clear-cut victory for the North. The Confederate invasion had been turned back, but an opportunity to destroy Lee's army had been missed.

Continuing your hike, follow a paved pathway for the first 200 meters. From there you, unlike Pickett's men, must follow a path through the fields. Don't walk through any crops. (The fields were wheat in 1863; they are now milo, because wheat has proved irresistible to the overabundant deer herd in the park.)

On the path, you will find a couple of missing rails in the fence next to Emmittsburg Road. Cross carefully. (Traffic was one hazard Pickett's men didn't have to face that day.) There is a gap in the fence on the other side. Follow the path to the Angle, cross the low stone wall, and continue across Hancock Avenue to the High Water Mark Trail. Bear left and make your way back to the Cyclorama Center.

After you've seen the museum, you can find additional hiking on the 5.6 km Johnny Reb Trail. See the *Gettysburg Heritage Trail Guide* for directions.

8

Sunset Rocks

Location: 8 miles south of exit 37 off I-81

Distance: 13.3 km (8.3 miles)

Time: 5 hours

Vertical rise: 323 meters (1,060 feet)

Highlights: View

Maps: USGS 7½' Dickinson; PATC map 2–3

This hike on the famous Appalachian Trail (AT) and the Sunset Rocks side trail is based at Pine Grove Furnace State Park. The camp store at this park, which you will pass as you drive in, is the site of the half-gallon club. AT through-hikers are expected to buy, and consume on the spot, half a gallon of ice cream. Not to worry: Through-hikers expend 4,000, 5,000, or more calories per day and lose at least 10 kg along the way. Don't try this if you're not a through-hiker!

There are rocks, wet spots, stream crossings, and usually some mud along this hike, so you will want your hiking boots.

How to Get There

Pine Grove Furnace State Park is located on PA 233, 8.1 miles south of exit 37 off I-81 (found between Carlisle and Shippensburg). It is 13.5 miles northeast of US 30 at Caledonia State Park. From the north, turn right at the park office and then take the second left, passing the park store (formerly the stable of the old ironworks). Turn left twice again, passing the furnace stack and parking there. From the west, turn right onto Bendersville Lane at the park boundary, passing the AYH hostel, formerly the ironmaster's mansion. Turn right and then left to reach the furnace stack. Avoid the area reserved for overnight hikers on the AT.

The Trail

From the furnace stack, follow the white blazes of the AT back across Bendersville Road and past the AYH hostel. Turn left onto PA 233 for 175 meters (use caution) and then turn right onto a gravel road. This is the AT, which climbs gently, passing several cabins and cottages. Continue climbing on a charcoal road. When the trail levels off, you pass several hearths where charcoal was made for the iron furnace back at Pine Grove. The trail becomes rockier, passing young white pines and then descending to an unsigned junction with the blue-blazed Sunset Rocks Trail at 2.7 km. You will return on this trail toward the end of this hike. For now, cross Toms Run on a footbridge and continue on Old Shippensburg Road. Farther along, this road is still passable to vehicles and is used to reach camps near the AT. At 3.1 km a side trail leads left to a spring.

There is a power line along this road. Where the power line turns right, so do you. Camp Michaux was once located to your left; in the 1930s it was the first Civilian Conservation Corps camp in the state. During World War II it served as a prisoner-of-war camp; after the war it became a church camp. Many early meetings of the Keystone Trails Association were held here,

before it was abandoned in 1972.

Now pass the stone ruins of a barn behind a fringe of spruce trees. This barn is said to have been built by Hessian prisoners during the Revolution.

Continue ahead on Old Shippensburg Road. At 4.3 km turn left onto a gated old woods road. Red, white, and chestnut oaks grow along this section of the trail. In places there is an understory of white pines, which are not supposed to be shade-tolerant.

Bear left and cross a stream as best you can. At 6.1 km you reach the Toms Run Shelters. Shelters are a tradition on the AT, dating back to the days of heavy canvas tents and frameless packs. Today there are more than 200 such shelters along the trail. Building and maintaining them at remote sites such as this absorbs an enormous amount of volunteer effort: A new shelter may require 3,000 volunteer days. It certainly is a great relief to reach a shelter after an all-day rain, but through-hikers must still carry a tent. The shelters are not evenly spaced along the AT, and there may be gaps of up to 50 km between them. When you do reach a shelter it may already be full, as they

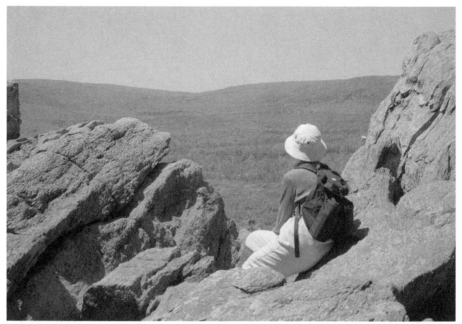

The view from Sunset Rocks

operate on a first-come, first-served basis. Further, the shelters have become magnets for trail problems. For instance, in theory occupancy is limited to a single night, but you may find a youth group that stays a fortnight. (It's a lot cheaper for the group than going to a commercial summer camp.)

The Toms Run Shelters make a convenient place to stop for lunch. Then move on, crossing the outlet from a spring and then a bridge over Toms Run. Just beyond, turn left onto the blue-blazed Sunset Rocks Trail. Again, there is no sign. (The AT is poorly signed—not because signs haven't been made and installed, but because they've been stolen or destroyed by vandals.)

Soon you cross a wet spot and then pass a clear-cut to your right that has grown into a thick stand of black birch. Beyond it is another cut to your left that has grown into red maple. Pass several char-

coal flats, then continue on a logging road. At 7.3 km bear right in a clearing. This junction is poorly blazed even when leaves are off the trees. Cross some wet areas and then turn right onto paved Michaux Road.

After 300 meters turn left onto the second of two gravel roads. (The blazes are confusing at this point and seem to indicate a turn on the first side road.) Continue on the trail and circle a camp. The trail parallels the ridge before turning right and climbing to the crest of Little Rocky Ridge. As you proceed east, the path becomes a scramble over rock outcrops. Follow the blazes as best you can.

This ridge has a rugged beauty and is set about with white and pitch pines in addition to chestnut oaks. At 9.5 km you reach a trail junction in a sag. To reach the view, continue ahead to the east end of Little Rocky Ridge. You will be looking south and west.

Return to the sag and turn right (north) on the trail. Descend—steeply, at first—passing a stand of hemlocks to a junction with the AT at 10.5 km. Turn right onto the AT and retrace your steps to the park and your car.

9

Cumberland Valley

Location: Between Carlisle and Mechanicsburg

Distance: 16.5 km (10.3 miles)

Time: 4¾ hours

Vertical rise: 135 meters (450 feet)

Highlights: Rural Pennsylvania

Maps: USGS 7½' Mechanicsburg, Carlisle, Wertzville; PATC map 1

Cumberland Valley is the local name for the Great Valley of the Appalachians, running from Georgia to New York State. When the Appalachian Trail (AT) was first laid out back in the 1930s, the Cumberland Valley was completely rural. The AT was routed on un-paved roads across the valley, whose cross-ing is a matter of geographic necessity since South Mountain comes to an abrupt end just north of Dillsburg.

After World War II the valley began to change. Suburbs and industry spread out from Harrisburg, and roads were paved. Much of the land remained rural but was hidden from the roads by a veneer of devel-opment. Traffic became fast and heavy. The AT experience was seriously eroded–de-spite people like the ice cream lady, who gave ice cream to passing hikers.

Volunteers enlisted the National Park Service as empowered under the National Scenic Trail Act to purchase a corridor of land to get the AT off the roads. Several al-ternative routes were investigated. The route finally selected follows Stony Ridge, which runs straight across the valley. One of the leaders of this effort was Craig Dunn of Camp Hill.

Stony Ridge results from a vertical layer of igneous rock (originally molten) called a diabase dike. This dike is also responsible for the "boiling springs" of Boiling Springs: The igneous rock is impervious to ground-water, forcing it to the surface.

Wear your boots for this hike, as there are stones on Stony Ridge, and there may be a good deal of mud. Be sure to stick to the trail; the public-use corridor is only 30 meters wide in places. Don't expect the wilderness experience typical of the AT. This section has a charm all its own.

How to Get There

This is a car-shuttle hike, so you'll need two cars. Take exit 52 off I-81 between Harrisburg and Carlisle. Head "south" on US 11. Immediately after the Budget Host Motel and across from Howard Johnson's, turn right onto Country Club Road. Drive east for 2.1 miles and turn left onto Bernheisel Road at a T-junction. Drive north for 0.9 mile, crossing over Conodoguinet Creek. Then turn left into Scott Farm, the Mid-Atlantic Trail Crew headquarters. (Hiking is spoken here.)

Leave one car at Scott Farm and retrace your route to US 11. Turn right and get into the left lane as quickly as you can. After just 0.4 mile turn left onto Middlesex Road at "Mature Fantasy." Drive south for 6.1 miles, crossing PA 641 at grade, zigzagging at Lisburn Road, and crossing PA 74 where the road name changes to South Ridge Road. At PA 174 turn right; 0.2 mile brings you to the Appalachian Trail Conference's (ATC) Mid-Atlantic Regional Office across from Farmers Trust Bank. Turn left into the small parking lot. You may have to park elsewhere in Boiling Springs if this lot is full.

The Trail

From the ATC office, cross First Street (PA 174) and turn right. The 5 by 15 cm white blazes show that you are on the AT. Walk on the left, facing traffic, and climb the low hill, crossing South Ridge Road. After 400 meters turn left onto a mowed path through a field of goldenrod. Some of these fields are returning to woods. Tens of thousands of pines and oaks have been planted by volunteers, to screen the AT from future de-

velopment. The blazes are painted on wooden posts in the absence of both trees and large rocks.

At 1.1 km you enter a patch of woods, but soon you're back in the fields. Many of the fields on national park land are rented by farmers. Any appropriate, established use can be continued—growing corn or soybeans, or pasturing cows or horses. The intent is to preserve the agricultural character of the AT corridor.

The land is gently rolling and South Mountain, the southern edge of Cumberland Valley, can be seen behind you from the tops of rises. At several places farm roads cross the trail. It takes 7 or 8 days to mow the entire Cumberland Valley section of the AT. A lot more work is required to maintain a trail in the open than one in the woods. The trail must be mowed almost continuously during the growing season.

At 2.4 km you cross an old stone wall, and at 3.2 km you cross PA 74. Be careful. There is some parking on the far side. Then cross a stile over an electric fence and make your way across a horse pasture. Cross another stile at the far side of the pasture. (A stile is preferable to a gate in a fence, as it can't be left open.)

Trees along the trail are locust, walnut, both black cherry and chokecherry, mulberry, birch, and even a stray white pine.

Cross Lisburn Road at 4.8 km. Now turn right, enter woods, and turn left onto an old paved road. At 5.8 km cross Boyer Road, which is also paved. Then cross a wet area and a bridge over a small stream. Cross PA 641 (Trindle Road) at 6.5 km. Again, be careful—lots of high-speed traffic. At 8.3 km, cross Ridge Road, also paved, followed by a footbridge.

Next, you pass a small pond, which may have wild ducks, and cross a footbridge over the outlet. Cross Old Stone House

Puncheon

Road at 9.2 km and climb over a high stile. At the far edge of the field is a small cemetery—the Chambers (of Chambersburg) family cemetery.

Switchback up a rock slope at 10 km, cross another paved road, and cross an unpaved road. Then turn left onto the next hard-surfaced road. Cross the Pennsylvania Turnpike on the road bridge at 10.7 km.

Turn left just beyond a house and follow the edge of a field to a crossing of the Conrail tracks. Do check for trains—although most of the heavy traffic is now on the roads. Continue through fields and woods, crossing US 11 on a footbridge at 12.6 km. (Before the AT relocation, hikers had to cross US 11 at grade.)

After more fields and woods, turn left onto paved Bernheisel Road and cross I-81 on the road bridge at 14.1 km. Then bear right into a field. You come to the junction of Bernheisel and Country Club Roads at 14.8 km. Blue Mountain, the northern edge of Cumberland Valley, looms directly ahead.

Cross a stile into a cow pasture. Watch for blazes carefully here, as there are only a few of them. The blazed posts are circled by small fences to protect them from marauding cows.

After two more stiles turn right, cross a footbridge, and enter woods along Conodoguinet Creek. The AT is cut into the slope below Bernheisel Road. This is followed by a section of puncheon, which is occasionally rearranged or even swept away by floods.

At 16.3 km turn left onto Bernheisel Road and cross Conodoguinet Creek. Finally, turn left into Scott Farm, where you left one of your cars.

If development continues at its present rate, the AT corridor will soon be the only open green space left in the Cumberland Valley. If you would like to get involved in the efforts to maintain the AT experience, you can join the Cumberland Valley Appalachian Trail Management Association, P.O. Box 395, Boiling Springs, PA 17007.

Additional hiking opportunities can be found on the AT. To the north you can hike all the way to Mount Katahdin in Maine; to the south you can hike to Springer Mountain in Georgia.

An artist created this chain-saw sculpture from a tree stump that was left behind after a Pennsylvania Bureau of Forestry project. It's found along the Capital Area Greenbelt, directly behind the county prison.

10

Joseph E. Ibberson
State Conservation Area

*Location: Peters Mountain north
of Harrisburg*

Distance: 4.9 km (3.0 miles)

Vertical rise: 240 meters (790 feet)

Highlights: A walk in the woods

Maps: USGS 7½' Enders; park map

What's the difference between a state conservation area and a state park? A conservation area offers a variety of environmental education and interpretive programs. Riding of horses, bicycles, and motorized devices is not permitted. State parks, on the other hand, provide picnic areas, campgrounds, swimming areas, and boating.

This 140-hectare tract belonged to Joseph Ibberson, a graduate of the Yale School of Forestry. Ibberson bought up this land over the years and thought of it as a tree farm, but in 1998 he donated the parcel to the state of Pennsylvania. He worked for the Pennsylvania Bureau of Forestry up to his retirement in 1977.

Some of the trails here are rocky; you will appreciate your hiking boots, although this hike could be done with walking shoes. The trails are well blazed, and there are signs at many junctions. Rest rooms and water are available at the parking lot.

How to Get There

The conservation area is located on the north flank of Peters Mountain in Dauphin County, north of Harrisburg. To reach Ibberson from the north on PA 147, turn onto PA 225 and drive south through Matamoras for 1.6 miles. Then turn left onto Hebrun Road and drive 4.7 miles to a large sign at the main entrance. From the south, drive north on PA 225 from US 322 for 4.5 miles, then turn right onto Hebrun Road.

10. Joseph Ibberson

Ⓟ Appalachian Trail

Ⓟ Parking

N

0		1/2 mile

0		1/2 kilometer

The Trail

To start your hike, head into the woods on the red-blazed Evergreen Trail. In a few steps turn left onto a logging road. At 120 meters you reach a junction with the Pine Trail and the blue-blazed Victoria Trail. Continue on the Victoria Trail and start to climb. Pass several unblazed trails to your left. Note how the hemlocks have been devastated by the woolly adelgid, an aphid that sucks the juices out of hemlock needles. It was accidentaly introduced from Japan some years ago. Efforts have been made to control it with ladybugs. The woolly adelgid

produces whitish masses on hemlock needles, which are most easily seen on the undersides of small branches.

Mountain laurel grows to a considerable height along the trail. In the early 1980s the oaks were defoliated by the gypsy moth. This permitted sunlight to reach the forest floor and resulted in the germination of white pine seeds. Many of these seedlings can be seen in the understory. Will they continue to grow and push aside the large hardwoods that currently dominate this forest or will they become stunted, sickly, and eventually die?

At 350 meters the Evergreen Trail turns right, but you continue following the blue blazes. After climbing over some rocks you reach the edge of a "bench" and descend briefly, crossing the Rock Trail. Bear right on an old road at 0.9 km. This is the old Victoria Trail, which led across Peters Mountain to Victoria Iron Furnace in Clark Valley and not to a lingerie outlet. The climb continues, passing a junction with the Whitetail Trail, which you will take on the way back.

Toward the top, the trail is flanked with dead and dying hemlocks—more victims of the woolly adelgid. There is no water table this far up the ridge, so trees growing here are already stressed. What will replace these hemlocks? Is this forest an ongoing process or a mass extinction without an asteroid? There are some leaves-off views to the north. At 1.8 km irregular white blazes mark the boundary of the conservation area, and at 2 km you reach a gate and junction with the Appalachian Trail (AT). Turn left toward Maine. This hike turns back at the point where the Victoria Trail turns right and descends to PA 325. You could extend your trek by following the AT to the boundary of State Game Lands 211 in about 0.7 km or descend Peters Mountain to PA 325 on the southern part of the Victoria Trail, but un-

---

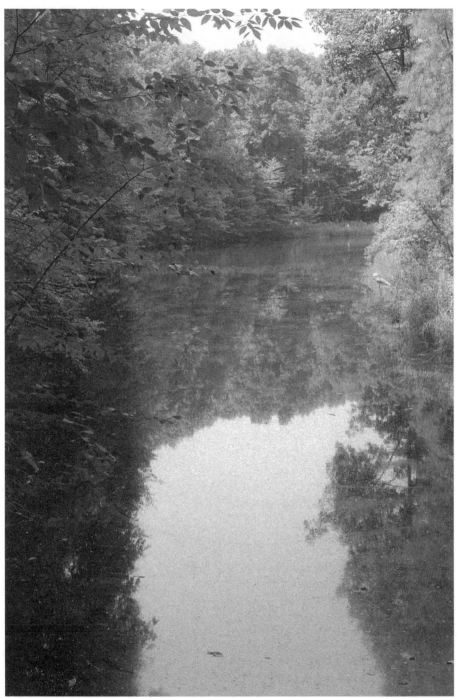

The pond on Whitetail Trail

less you left a car there, you'd have to re-climb the mountain on your way back. There is a view of Clark Creek Valley a couple hundred meters farther south on Victoria Trail.

Turn right at the gate and retrace your steps to the pink-blazed Whitetail Trail. Turn left and continue downhill, keeping left where the Sawmill Trail comes in. Ignore several unblazed old roads, continuing on Whitetail when Sawmill turns right. Pass a small pond and cross the Pine Trail, reaching the edge of the bench. To the west of here, near Clarks Ferry, this bench is more prominent.

Descend and continue ahead at a confusing trail junction at 4.2 km. When you see private land ahead, turn right at a gate and follow the red blazes of the Evergreen Trail. Pass two more gates to the left and then turn left on trail to the parking lot.

Additional hiking opportunities can be found on the many trails, blazed and unblazed, here on the lower slopes of Peters Mountain not used by this hike.

11

Wildwood Lake

Location: Northern edge of Harrisburg

Distance: 5.3 km (3.4 miles)

Time: 2 hours

Vertical rise: 20 meters (65 feet)

Highlights: Lake, wildlife, nature center

Maps: USGS 7½' Harrisburg West; KTA sections 7 and 8

11. Wildwood Lake

Ⓟ Parking

N

0 _____ 1/2 mile

0 _____ 1/2 kilometer

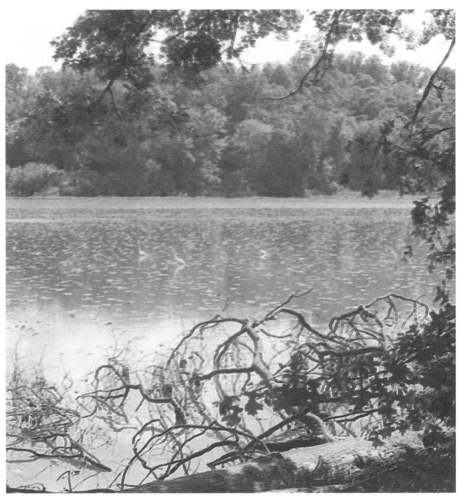
Wildwood Lake

Wildwood Lake is a shallow lake created by damming Paxton Creek on the north side of Harrisburg early in the 20th century. The lake is bounded by PA 39 on the north, US 322 on the east, I-81 on the south, and Industrial Road on the west, yet it is surprisingly wild if you can ignore the traffic and other industrial noise pollution. In 1999 the Olewine Nature Center was added in the southeast corner of the area. You can follow this trail with walking shoes or even sneakers.

How to Get There

There are three parking areas along Industrial Road and another one at the nature center. This hike can be taken from any of these areas, as it circles the lake. From the north, it is just 0.2 mile from the junction of Industrial Road and PA 39 where the latter crosses over US 322. From the south, Industrial Road starts at the north parking lot for the Pennsylvania Farm Show on US 322. Follow Industrial Road past

Harrisburg Area Community College and under I-81 to any of the four parking lots. This description begins at the northernmost lot of Industrial Road near PA 39.

The Hike

From the picnic shelter, bear right on the wood-chipped Tow Path Trail. If this towpath indeed followed a real canal in the 19th century, it must now be submerged in the lake. Pin oaks, maples, and locusts grow along the towpath, together with poison ivy. Swallows hunt flying insects low over the water, while a family of ducks crosses the towpath to the backwater. Egrets stalk frogs and fish in the shallow water. The egrets nest on islands in the nearby Susquehanna River, but a "recreational" dam has been proposed that would flood these islands, destroying the nesting area. Greenbrier grows along the shore, while yellow water lilies—the American version of the lotus—fill the lake and backwater. The path is complete with mileposts.

At 1.9 km turn left at the parking lot. There are rest rooms and a water fountain. Here you join the Capital Area Greenbelt, which you will explore more fully in Hike 12. The greenbelt emerges from under I-81 and follows the lakeshore on the paved trail past Morning Glory Spillway. Several spotting scopes are found along this section. Red-winged blackbirds call from the cattail stalks.

Pass a mapboard and turn left at 2.2 km onto the Delta Trail—a boardwalk through the marsh that features a drawbridge at the start. The Olewine Nature Center is just a few meters to your right at the top of the rise. Back on the Delta Trail, pass a display on animal identification. At 2.5 km there is a lookout to your left in a waterfowl nesting area. In the woods, shade is provided by box elders. Cross another drawbridge and turn left onto the gravel road, briefly rejoining the Capital Area Greenbelt and crossing Paxton Creek on the bridge. Bear left but avoid the North Boardwalk, which is a dead end.

Instead, bear left at 2.9 km on the East Shore Trail, where bikes are prohibited. This is a real trail with a dirt footway (occasionally mud). There are some wet spots.

Sycamore, tulip tree, hickory, and ash grow along this section. Mayapples cover the forest floor. At 4.3 km turn left onto paved Wildwood Way. You'll find a picnic table and a Porta-Potti here. Cross Fox Run but ignore the Fox Run Trail to your left. Here the Wildwood Trail is shaded by basswood. Next, the trail climbs to a bench with a view across the lake. It then passes Susquehanna Spillway and some mulberry trees to reach the parking lot where you started.

Additional hiking opportunities at Wildwood Lake can be found on the North Boardwalk, Tall Timbers, and Fox Run Trails. You could also visit the nature center, which has lots of hands-on exhibits for kids.

12

Capital Area Greenbelt

Location: Southern edge of Harrisburg

Distance: 5.5 km (3.4 miles)

Time: 1¾ hours

Vertical rise: 20 meters (70 feet)

Highlights: Urban greenway

Maps: USGS 7½' Harrisburg East, Steelton; Greenbelt brochure

The Capital Area Greenbelt owes its existence to Mira Lloyd Dock (1853–1945). Dock was a formidable Victorian lady. In an era when almost no women went to college, and after being out of school for 20 years, she enrolled at the University of Michigan in 1896, taking botany, chemistry, and geology. Those acquainted with the struggle over Hetch Hetchy Valley in California will appreciate that Dock knew both Gifford Pinchot and John Muir. In 1900 she informed the Harrisburg Board of Trade that the town needed an "emerald necklace"— the Capital Area Greenbelt. When completed, that necklace will be 32 km long.

With Dock's death in 1945, work on the Greenbelt faltered, but it was revived in the 1990s by Norman Lacasse, Carl Lorentz, and Shirley and Sid Disend when greenways came back into fashion. Lorentz defines the greenbelt as "a system of linear parks that has a trail." Private land problems have thus far foiled its completion.

The greenbelt is *not* a wilderness footpath. It is paved either with fine gravel or blacktop. Walking shoes or even sneakers are fine here. Residents of the Harrisburg area are fortunate to have this unique opportunity for recreation and relaxation—no other town in Pennslvania has anything like it—and they can be found here in droves during their lunch breaks and after work. There are also plenty of birds along the greenbelt, and too many deer. This hike follows its southerly portion, from South Bridge on I-83 to the Five Senses Garden

12. Capital Area Greenbelt

N

Ⓟ Parking

0 ——————— 1/2 mile

0 ——————— 1/2 kilometer

on PA 441. It is described as a car shuttle but could be completed as an in-and-out hike due to its short length.

How to Get There

First make your way to the parking lot across from the Five Senses Garden on PA 441 south of Paxton Street and next to Spring Creek. This location is just west of East Mall and the county prison. Cross the new bridge over Spring Creek. Park one car here. In your other car turn left onto PA 441, but continue ahead in a block where PA 441 turns off. At 0.3 mile turn left onto Paxton Street at a traffic light. Pass under I-83 and cross PA 230. Bear right on Second Street, but keep left. At 2.2 miles turn left onto Washington Street, then left again onto South Front Street. Keep right on this street, avoiding Race Street. Pass under South Bridge and turn right to park under the bridge, for a total of 2.9 miles.

The Hike

To start your hike, find the trail next to the Susquehanna River's bank. The trail is un-

Susquehanna River

marked save for occasional signs, but you'll have little difficulty in following it. Upstream you can see several bridges as well as the Dock Street Dam, but turn downstream, passing many memorial trees. This is recycled land; about 20 cm under the surface there is a layer of slag from four iron furnaces. The tree roots can grow out but not down.

At 460 meters turn right onto a road next to the Penn DOT building and continue past a gate where there is a cutoff to your left. This is more recycled land, littered with old paving blocks. The trail next swings left at Paxton Creek, then parallels the railroad.

At 1.4 km turn sharply right and cross the railroad on a steel bridge where the cutoff comes in from your left. Follow the trail around a bend under a railroad bridge. Then cross a bridge over a stream. This part of the path is shaded. Beware of poison ivy if you stray off the trail, which now parallels Cameron Street. Pass a parking lot at 2.9 km and cross Cameron Street. Be careful.

Quigley's Restaurant is a block to your left. Here you can buy sandwiches and select from a variety of beers on tap. There are also rest rooms. Such facilities are scarce along the greenbelt.

Back on the trail, pass a gate and follow a paved road along Spring Creek, crossing the creek first on a stone bridge and then on a concrete one. Trees along the trail are sycamore, chokecherry, basswood, mulberry, and box elder. Note the deer fence around the carefully tended vegetable gardens next to an apartment block. Pass another parking lot and then go under a bridge on 19th Street. Bear right on a gated road at 4.2 km. At 4.8 km there is a bird identification display.

Next, reach the parking lot on PA 441 (28th Street) where you left your car. Cross the highway to reach the Five Senses Garden. Plantings are designed to stimulate smell, sight, touch, sound, and taste; for sound, you will have to listen to the waters of Spring Creek. The safety of all plants in the taste garden can't be guaranteed, because strangers have planted some unknown specimens. Note how heavily the rhododendrons and mountain laurel have been browsed by deer. The garden was built on the site of a former dump.

Before the new PA 441 bridge was built, three culverts carried Spring Creek under the highway. In times of flood they proved inadequate, and the garden area was flooded repeatedly.

For additional hiking opportunities in Harrisburg, follow the greenbelt north along the Susquehanna River past the Dock Street Dam and some of the bridges. The trail follows the riverbank for about 6 km.

13

Peters Mountain

Location: North of Harrisburg, at the US 322 bridge over the Susquehanna River

Distance: 7.6 km (4.7 miles)

Time: 4 hours

Vertical rise: 315 meters (1030 feet)

Highlights: Views, AT shelters

Maps: USGS 7½' Halifax, Duncannon; KTA sections 7 and 8

Since the Appalachian Trail (AT) was completed in the mid-1930s, much of it has been relocated. Then there have been relocations of the relocations; in some places the trail has actually been relocated to its original route. On Peters Mountain you will see evidence of three different trail locations, each one better than the previous. The original location of the AT wasn't even on Peters Mountain, but on Blue Mountain just above Harrisburg. The Blue Mountain site required an extensive detour in order to cross the Susquehanna, so in 1955 the trail was relocated by Earl Shaffer, the first AT through-hiker, to cross on the Clarks Ferry Bridge.

There are only a few wet spots along this hike, but there are rocks, lots of rocks, so wear your hiking boots.

How to Get There

The trailhead is at the south end of the Clarks Ferry Bridge (US 322) over the Susquehanna River. From either direction, exit onto PA 147 and park off the pavement after you see the APPALACHIAN TRAIL sign. This point is 1.9 miles from the intersection of US 11/US 15 with US 322 on the far side of the river, at Amity Hall.

The Trail

Walk back to the APPALACHIAN TRAIL sign and follow the white blazes across the live railroad. Look for trains before you cross. Use the end of a stone wall as a stairway and continue through a couple of switchbacks, the first of which involves an old utility pole. When I saw this trail, its fine quality made me think it

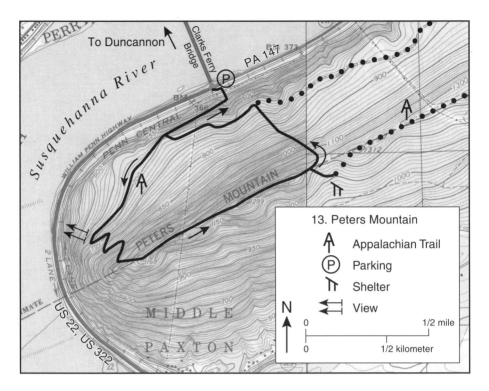

13. Peters Mountain

⚑ Appalachian Trail
Ⓟ Parking
⛺ Shelter
⇆ View

N

0 ————————————— 1/2 mile
0 ————————————— 1/2 kilometer

must have been built by the Mid-Atlantic Trail Crew—but it is the work of one man, Ron Gray, plus the occasional helpers he dragooned into service. Some rockwork farther on was done by the Mid-Atlantic Trail Crew.

Note the poison ivy along the trail. Poison ivy is locally abundant on Peters Mountain. Locust, sassafras, maple, and red oak also grow here.

This section of the AT is blazed in accordance with a standard adopted by the Appalachian Trail Conference in 1995: Double blazes are used; at turns, the upper blaze is displaced in the direction that the trail takes.

Farther up, the AT follows the base of a ledge before finding a passage through it. There is an intersection on your left with the blue-blazed Susquehanna Trail, on which you will return. A few steps farther an unblazed trail leads right, to a previous loca-

tion of the AT, which was too steep and started to erode.

Continue on the bench, passing a stone wall and, at 1.1 km, a stone foundation to the left of the trail. These are the remains of a farm here, on the bench halfway up Peters Mountain. Pass a spring and turn right onto an old woods road.

At 1.6 km you reach a view over Duncannon, the Susquehanna, and Cove Mountain on the other side of this water gap. Now climb up the crest of the ridge on a series of switchbacks to some big rocks at 2.4 km. There is a view downstream from the top of the first big rock.

At the top of the ridge, continue on good footway to another view: At the point where the trail crosses to the other side of the ridge, you can see the Clarks Ferry Bridge. The rocks along the ridgetop are conglomerate, which looks like con-

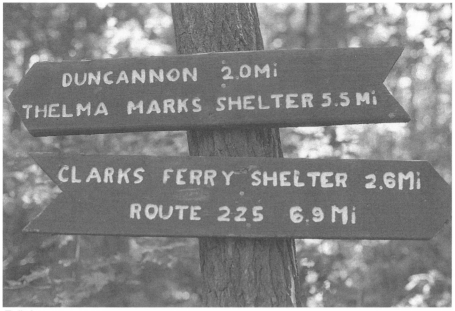

Trail signs

crete because it is full of pebbles. Conglomerate is actually a very coarse sandstone. This is the Pocono sandstone of the Mississippian age. Along with the Tuscarora and Pottsville sandstones, it is one of the chief ridge-formers in eastern Pennsylvania.

Ahead, the ridge becomes a rockpile; you must follow blazes carefully. This very rough section continues for 700 meters.

At 4 km you reach a junction with the blue-blazed Susquehanna Trail. Pass it by for now to visit the Clarks Ferry Shelter, built in 1987. The AT drops off the ridgetop. Turn right at a signed junction at 4.5 km and follow the obvious trail to the shelter.

This shelter is made of lumber and has a wooden floor, a shingle roof, bunks, a picnic table, and an outhouse, all set in a small clearing. This means you can dry your things—if the sun comes out. The Peters Mountain Shelter, built in 1994 on the other side of PA 225, makes this one look primi-tive. Peters Mountain is much larger, with a sleeping loft and a solar composting out-house. Despite more than 200 shelters along the AT, through-hikers must still carry tarps or tents. Sometimes shelters are filled beyond capacity, and there are gaps of up to 50 km between them.

To continue your hike, walk back up to the AT and bear left. At the junction with the blue-blazed trail, turn sharply right along the ridgetop. Turn sharply left at a stone cairn and start down the side of Peters Mountain. Side trails don't get the same level of care as the main AT, but this one is fairly straight, which is helpful if you have to detour around blowdowns. There are lots of loose rocks, so watch your step. This trail crosses private land and so could be closed at any time by the landowners.

On the bench you pass the site of the old Clarks Ferry Shelter at 5.7 km. This shelter was removed due to improper use. The spring is off to your right.

Peters Mountain

Follow the blue blazes down to a woods road and bear left on it. This woods road is also a former route of the AT. Cross the yellow-blazed national park boundary and continue on the sparsely blazed woods road to 6.3 km. (In many places the AT is now a long, skinny national park, maintained and managed by volunteers.)

Turn right on trail. Cross the swath of an old pole line, with another view of the Clarks Ferry Bridge. Continue along the top of a ledge to the break used by the AT. Here, turn sharply right and descend the impressive sidehill construction to PA 147 and your car.

For additional hiking on Peters Mountain, you could follow the AT farther "north" from the Clarks Ferry Shelter. The sidewalk on the Clarks Ferry Bridge is far safer than its predecessor, but I can't recommend it on aesthetic grounds: Monster trucks rumble right by your elbow.

14

Stone Tower Trail

Location: On PA 325 between Dauphin and Tower City

Distance: 12.1 km (7.5 miles)

Time: 5½ hours

Vertical rise: 395 meters (1,300 feet)

Highlights: Large wild area

Maps: USGS 7½' Grantville, Lykens; KTA sections 7 and 8

Just 20 kilometers north of the state capital is Saint Anthony's Wilderness, the second largest roadless area in Pennsylvania. The origin and significance of the name are lost in time. It appears on maps from before the Revolution.

During the 19th century the area was a center of extractive industry. Coal mining, iron making, and logging left the ridges bare and the streams polluted with acid mine drainage. The area is haunted by ghost towns of that era (there are said to be more than 1,000 ghost towns in Pennsylvania), including Rattling Run, Yellow Springs, Gold Mine Gap Station, Cold Spring, and Rausch Gap. A standard-gauge railroad, the Schuylkill & Susquehanna (S&SRR), ran the length of Stony Valley between Second and Stony Mountains, linking these towns with the outside world.

As in much of Pennsylvania, this land was used and abused, but it has rebounded. The railroad is gone, forests again cover the ridges, and Stony Creek has been brought back to life by neutralizing the acid drainage with crushed limestone at Rausch Gap. Saint Anthony's Wilderness is now incorporated into State Game Lands 211; it stretches from near the Susquehanna east past Swatara Gap.

Sheer size makes Saint Anthony's Wilderness difficult to hike. Access from the south is restricted by private land and the Indiantown Gap Military Reservation, which uses the south side of Second Mountain as the impact area for artillery practice.

Access from PA 325 in Clarks Valley is limited by the De Hart Reservoir and Stony Mountain. The easiest access is from the ends of the S&SRR grade at Ellendale Forge and Gold Mine Road, or via the Appalachian Trail (AT).

This is a short but rugged hike based on the PA 325 access. You will certainly want your hiking boots for the boulder slopes and a few wet spots. This should not be your first hike, as parts of it are rugged and there is a critical turn.

How to Get There

The trailhead is on PA 325, 5 miles east of the De Hart Dam. There is no trail sign, just a big red blaze on a tree facing west, but the trailhead is bracketed by small signs saying SR 325/370 on the west and SR 325/390 on the east. If you find a blue- or yellow-marked trailhead, you are too far east by 0.9 or 2.0 miles, respectively. There is parking space for only two cars at the trailhead, but there are more pulloffs in both directions along the highway.

The Trail

Head into the woods on the obvious footway, following neatly made red blazes. Turns use the offset double blaze adopted by the Appalachian Trail Conference in 1995; the upper blaze is displaced in the direction of the turn.

At 200 meters, cross Clark Creek on a log; there's a steel cable to hold on to.

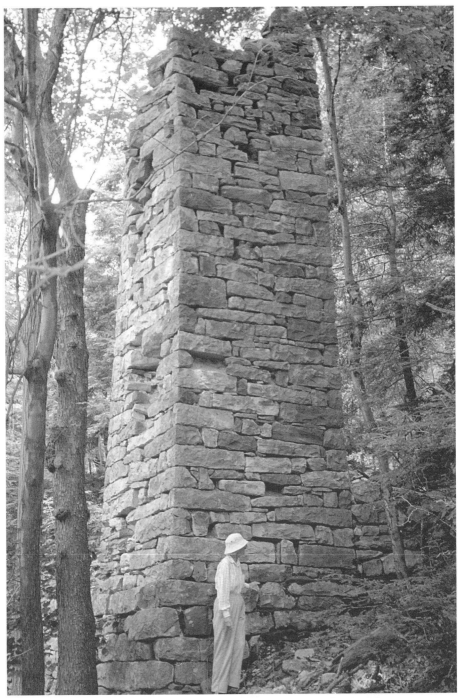

Stone tower

Boards have been nailed to the top of the log, improving the footing, but if you can't reach the cable you may have to ford the creek or get a companion to hold down the cable while you cross. Turn right onto an old road at 700 meters. To your left this old road, on which you will return, is blazed pink.

At 1.1 km turn left and climb on an old grade, passing the white-blazed boundary of Game Lands 211. Next, turn right onto another old road that holds to the contour. Turn left onto a log skid at 1.9 km for some serious climbing. The log skid evaporates after 100 meters and you bear right up a boulder scree, with occasional red blazes but no trace of footway. There are only 110 meters of this scree slope before you reach the end of an old road, but there seem to be many more.

Turn right onto the old road and continue to climb, passing a spring at 2.3 km. Note the dry stone walls on the side of this road; somebody put a lot of work into them but never finished—just another of the mysteries of Saint Anthony's Wilderness.

Swing left at the top of Stony Mountain to a junction with a blue-blazed trail at 3.3 km. Turn left. The red blazes continue to 3.5 km, where they turn right on a grassy bench among the workings of an old underground coal mine. The stone tower itself is partially hidden by trees. Beware: It looks as if it could collapse at any time. There is also an open vertical shaft. It is thought that the stone tower was used to create a draft, ventilating the mine shaft.

To continue your hike, follow the blue blazes down an old road to ruins of the ghost town of Yellow Springs. All that remain are piles of rock. Turn left onto the white-blazed AT, passing more ruins, then a spring. At 7.3 km turn left onto the blue-blazed Sand Spring Trail. There is a trail sign at this critical junction. Should you miss it, you may find an unmarked trail, right, to Cold Spring. Otherwise, you won't be sure something has gone wrong until the AT swings into Rausch Gap about 4 km from here.

Follow the Sand Spring Trail downhill and across the bright red waters of Rausch Creek. This is acid mine drainage, and it kills all life in the creek. At 7.8 km there is an unblazed side trail left, marked with a small wooden sign to THE GENERAL. The General (not included in this hike but only a 5-minute walk) turns out to be a rusting steam shovel used in coal stripping operations.

Bear right on the blue blazes for some serious climbing over Pottsville sandstone boulders to the top of Stony Mountain, and a junction with a yellow-blazed trail to the right, at 8.2 km. A sign painted on a rock at this junction advertises SOUTH VIEW, a 10-minute walk down the ridge. On a clear day you can see all the way to Reading, but the Yellow Trail is a blazed bushwhack innocent of all traces of clearing. It is not included in this hike.

Instead, continue straight ahead, passing a large hemlock, and start down the boulder scree. At 8.4 km you reach the end of a log skid, and the going gets easier. Sometimes blowdowns or trees force the trail off the log skid into the rough, but for the most part the path sticks to the grade. Farther down, some of the blue blazes have faded to white; you don't reach the game lands boundary, though, until 9.4 km.

Turn left onto the pink-blazed old road at 9.9 km. Sand Spring, a box spring set in moss-covered rocks, is within 20 meters of this junction. (You could reach PA 325 from here by staying with the blue blazes and rock-hopping across Clark Creek, but this would lead you to 1.4 km of tedious walking along the paved highway.)

Along the pink trail, pass a small boulder scree. You will reach the junction with the

Stone Tower Trail at 11.4 km. Turn right at the red blazes and follow them back across Clark Creek to PA 325, your starting point.

You can find additional hiking in Saint Anthony's Wilderness on the yellow-blazed trail you crossed or on a loop west of the De Hart Dam. Follow the AT up Stony Mountain to a junction with the Horse Shoe Trail; follow the Horse Shoe west to the Water Tank Trail. Turn right and follow either of two versions of the Water Tank Trail down Third Mountain. Then turn right again onto a blue-blazed trail that leads you back to the AT. See the KTA map, sections 7 and 8.

15

Swatara State Park

Location: Along I-81 north of Harrisburg

Distance: 18.0 km (11.2 miles)

Time: 5¾ hours

Vertical rise: 50 meters (170 feet)

Highlights: Swatara Creek, Waterville Bridge

Maps: USGS 7½' Tower City, Pine Grove, Indiantown Gap; park map

Swatara State Park is an undeveloped park between Blue and Second Mountains along I-81. The original intent was to dam Swatara Creek, creating a lake for water-oriented recreation, but the cost of the dam escalated relentlessly and Swatara is now to be developed as a trail park. I-81 borders one entire side, and you'd expect it to produce a full-throated roar throughout the park. On my visit, however, I was delighted to find that the noise pollution from this source was tolerable except near the Waterville Bridge. Elsewhere I could hear birdcalls, and I did not have to raise my voice to speak with companions.

This is a circuit hike around the park using the old state road on the southeast side of Swatara Creek and the old railroad grade on the opposite bank. This old grade is now designated the Swatara Multi-Use Trail and open to bicycles and horses as well as people. The old state road is also open to licensed motor vehicles, but as the pavement disintegrates, cars become limited in their speed. There are a few wet spots on the multiuse trail, but walking shoes should be adequate.

How to Get There

To reach the trailhead, take exit 100 off I-81 (old exit 31) and drive west on PA 443 for 2.1 miles. Then turn left onto Swopes Valley Road for 0.4 mile to a parking lot just across Swatara Creek and near Wagner's Pond.

The Trail

To start your hike, cross Swopes Valley Road and continue along the Old State

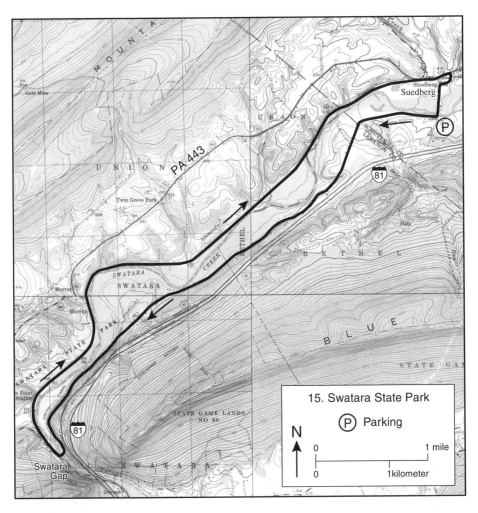

15. Swatara State Park

(P) Parking

N

0 — 1 mile
0 — 1 kilometer

Road next to Swatara Creek. Anglers park here. Despite some acid mine drainage, Swatara Creek harbors both trout and warmwater fish.

After a bit, Swatara Creek swings away from the road; you reach the fossil pit at 1 km. Marine fossils can be found in the Devonian shale exposed here, but you will need a hammer to crack open the rocks—and some patience as well.

The woods at Swatara are filled with dogwood that appears to have survived or avoided the blight. Next, the road crosses a meadow. White oak, tulip, and hickory trees are present. Hemlocks show the ravages of the woolly adelgid. Autumn olive is abundant. Poison ivy and Virginia creeper grow on the trees. At 2.9 km you enter a white pine woods. I-81 is very close but the roar is muted, at least when the leaves are out. Pass chestnut oak and basswood trees. A private holding, well plastered with NO TRESPASSING signs, is reached at 3.9 km.

You'll now encounter rhododendron growing under beech trees. These are very pleasant woods. Soon Swatara Creek be-

Swatara Creek

comes visible to your right, as do a number of roads that evidently lead to Swatara Creek. At 5.8 km you pass through a clearing followed by a gated road to your right. Wildflowers along the trail include mayapples, jack-in-the-pulpits, and wild azaleas.

A pipeline is encountered next to the road at 7.6 km. Shortly beyond is an old canal lift lock. The canal was a feeder branch for the Union Canal, used to bring anthracite coal from the mines to the north. The Swatara Canal was in service from 1832 to 1862, when a flood destroyed it—along with the reservoir that provided its water.

Next, at 8 km, you reach the cast-iron bridge over Swatara Creek. Built in 1890, it carried traffic across Little Pine Creek at Waterville until it was replaced by a two-lane bridge in the 1980s. The bridge was judged to be of historic value due to its lenticular truss design. Such historic bridges cannot be discarded when they are replaced. Efforts are made to find new homes for these structures, but if the efforts fail the bridge will just be set aside in a field.

The white-blazed Appalachian Trail (AT) uses the old bridge to cross Swatara Creek, and so do you. The AT goes up the bank on the far side, but you turn right onto the paved road. There is plenty of poison ivy to the side. Ignore a ramp that climbs to your left. Turn right onto the old railroad grade at 8.7 km just before an intersection with a paved road. The canal was not rebuilt after the flood of 1862 but was replaced by this railroad.

There is a paved road to your left, but it appears to be blocked to traffic. At 10.5 km the trail begins an extensive portion along Swatara Creek. River birch grows along the creek. Shortly after the site of Murry station the trail enters a rock cut, which continues until you reach some islands in Swatara Creek.

At 12.6 km you cross a road to a parking lot on your right; to your left it leads out to PA 443. Swatara Creek swings away, only to return again at 13.5 km. When it swings away it is followed by a meadow full of Virginia pines. At 14.8 the creek is back for a lengthy section. Some wild azaleas grow along the bank.

When the creek swings away again it is replaced by an open area; I hesitate to call this *meadow,* because hardly anything grows there. At 17 km the trail comes out to PA 443. Keep right for another 100 meters to where a trestle is missing. Then head out to PA 443 and continue along the highway. The railroad bridge over Mill Creek is missing, and this is the only way across. At 17.4 km turn right onto Swopes Valley Road and follow it across Swatara Creek to the parking lot for Wagner's Pond.

For additional hiking opportunities at Swatara State Park, follow the railroad grade east of Swopes Valley Road. It is about 2.5 km to the park boundary at I-81 near Irving Pond. Or you could follow the Appalachian Trail up onto Blue Mountain from the Waterville Bridge.

III

Philadelphia and Vicinity

The Wilderness Trail

16

Middle Creek

Location: 15 miles north of Lancaster

Distance: 5.3 km (3.3 miles)

Time: 2 hours

Vertical rise: 130 meters (490 feet)

Highlights: View, stream

Maps: USGS 7½' Womelsdorf, Richland; SGL 46 map 2

Middle Creek Wildlife Area was created primarily for one species—Canada geese. More than 250 other species of birds have been identified at Middle Creek as well, though. It is a birder's paradise. Middle Creek was dammed at a gap through the Furnace Hills, creating habitat for waterfowl. The balance of State Game Lands 46 is located on the Furnace Hills. Habitat doesn't have big brown eyes, but it's what really counts for wildlife.

The Horse Shoe Trail follows these hills across Middle Creek, and together with an old road and an abandoned trolley line it makes a small circuit hike on the east end of Black Oak Ridge.

A number of picnic areas are also provided on the 2,532 hectares of Middle Creek Wildlife Area, as well as a national-park-quality visitors center along the main road. Both Project 70 and Project 500 funds were used in the development of this area.

There are plenty of rocks and wet places, so wear your boots. There is also a lot of poison ivy along this hike.

How to Get There

The trailhead is on Hopeland Road (SR 2013), 3.1 miles south of the Hopeland/PA 897 intersection in Kleinfeltersville. You can also reach Middle Creek from US 322 at the village of Clay. Park along the road just north of the bridge over Middle Creek.

The Trail

Begin by heading up the yellow-blazed Horse Shoe Trail on the west side of the road. Soon you pass through a timber stand improvement cut. The haul roads have been seeded. At 700 meters you reach a junction with the Valley View Trail, which leads over the ridge and down to the Green Briar Picnic Area in about 1 km. The view over the wetlands is about 300 meters from this junction (not included in this hike). The Valley View Trail is marked with yellow metal triangles with one corner painted black; it is for foot travel only.

Continue up the Horse Shoe to a steel-pylon power line at 0.9 km. There is a view left across Middle Creek Gap. Beyond the power line, turn right onto an eroded old road that soon becomes a jeep road. Note that horses are permitted on this trail—but they would have to be very surefooted to negotiate the trail from the road to this point. This is the top of the hill. Next, you will see a food plot for game through the trees to your left; ordinarily, there isn't much for wildlife to eat in a mature forest.

At 1.5 km there is a view to the north across the power-line clearing. Turn left onto the Elders Run Trail at the bottom of the saddle, 1.9 km from the road. Note the spruce trees growing here.

Elders Run Trail is an old road gated to motor vehicles but open to horses. At 2.2 km there is an old stone springhouse to the right of the trail. Years ago, one of the shelters along the Horse Shoe Trail was located near this point. Shelters hold a magnetic attraction for vandals, but the Elders Run Shelter seems to have survived until as recently as 1987.

Farther along, you pass a cleared area that was probably a log landing. Then keep right on the main road to 3.3 km, where you cross a bridge over Elders Run. At 3.5 km turn sharply left onto the Middle Creek Trail, which appears to be an old railroad grade. Actually, it is an old trolley line that ran from Lancaster to Myerstown. This is now a foot-travel-only trail.

After repeated views of rapids in Middle Creek, cross a footbridge over Elders Run. A house on private land is visible on the far side of Middle Creek. Traverse a section of corduroy and pass a piped spring to the left of the trail at 4.4 km. Then pass under the power line and cross a couple of bridges, followed by a well-worn runaround (due to uncleared blowdowns on the old trolley grade). One more bridge and you are back at your car.

You can find additional hiking opportunities at Middle Creek on the Conservation and Willow Point Trails, both of which are quite short. Avoid the Deer Path Trail between the Red Rock and White Oak Picnic Areas unless it has been reopened.

There is also a short circuit hike east of Middle Creek. Climb the Millstone Trail from the White Oak Picnic Area, walking past the millstone to the vista over the lake. Head away from the vista and turn left onto an unmarked trail that leads to the Horse Shoe Trail. Turn right onto the Horse Shoe and follow it downhill to Middle Creek Gap. Turn right again onto Millstone Road and follow it back to the White Oak Picnic Area.

Finally, you could follow the Horse Shoe Trail to the west, to either Segloch Road or Fox Road; both options require a car shuttle.

17

Susquehannock State Park

Location: 20 miles south of Lancaster

Distance: 5.6 km (3.5 miles)

Time: 2¼ hours

Vertical rise: 220 meters (720 feet)

Highlights: Views, rhododendron

Maps: USGS 7½' Holtwood; park map

Susquehannock State Park, overlooking the lower Susquehanna River, is well developed for hiking, with 8 km of trails on only 91 hectares. This little-known park was listed by the Bureau of Parks as one of the 30 Best-Kept Secrets of Pennsylvania's State Parks. These parks are the least visited in the state. I find many of my favorites on this list.

You will find a mapboard of the park's trail system at one corner of the parking lot. The trails are coded with a rainbow of colors, including yellow, red, green, pink, beige, and magenta. On my first visit it appeared to me that the chromatically challenged were in for a tough time. Not to worry: There are no blazes of any color on the trails, so you are no worse off than anybody else in following them!

A problem with unmarked trails is that different people have different ideas of where the trail ought to go. If enough people are of the same mind, then a switchback may be cut off or a dead-end trail produced if people go straight where they should have turned. If you find yourself on a dead-end trail, turn back and try again.

Some of the trails above Wissler Run are steep, rocky, and slippery, so you will want your boots for this short hike.

How to Get There

Susquehannock Park can be reached by driving south 4.1 miles from PA 372 on Susquehannock Drive. Then turn right at a sign for the park and go 0.8 mile to a parking lot just beyond the Landis House.

The Trail

Walk between the old Landis House and the park office. Pick up the Rhododendron Trail near some rest rooms. Trail junctions are usually marked with post signs. At a junction, turn right onto the Five Points Trail and follow it over a footbridge. Then bear left uphill.

Along the trail you pass tulip, black gum, beech, black birch, chestnut oak, and wild holly. A small tree with big leaves growing luxuriantly along the trail is the pawpaw, which appears to be extending its range north from the Mason-Dixon line.

Next, turn left near the Five Points corner, where five different properties come together, and pass through dense stands of rhododendron. At 1.4 km turn left along Wissler Run and immediately cross a side stream. Then turn right onto the Rhododendron Trail and climb steeply. At 2 km turn left and continue climbing past tall banks of rhododendron (in bloom around the last week of June and the first week of July). Ignore a trail that goes ahead, as it doesn't go very far. Ignore another trail to your right at 2.4 km. The Rhododendron Trail climbs

Wissler Run

and descends frequently. Along this section note several stands of dead hemlocks that have been cut down. Presumably they were killed by the woolly adelgid.

Then, at 2.5 km, switchback to your left on an old grade and climb again, ignoring yet another trail to your right. At 2.7 km turn right onto the Fire Trail and follow it to an overlook above Wissler Run. This view is north to the Norman Wood Bridge, Lock 12 historic area, and Muddy Run pump storage plant.

Now turn back and climb on an old road to a picnic area with rest rooms. Keep right to another overlook at Hawk Point. The cliffs below you are more than 100 meters high. From here you can see some of the islands in the reservoir formed by the Conowingo Dam downstream in Maryland, as well as the Peach Bottom nuclear power station on the west side of the river. Mount Johnson Island was the first bald eagle sanctuary in the world.

From Hawk Point, proceed to a small parking lot, then continue on the Overlook Trail. At 3.8 km turn right onto the Landis Trail; shortly after, ignore a trail to your right. Next, turn right onto the Chimney Trail. At 4.6 km continue ahead on the Chimney Trail. The post sign is set wrong (or has been turned), and the trail that it indicates actually leads downhill to the park boundary.

Reach the end of the Pipe Line Trail and continue ahead on the Chimney Trail to the park road at 5.1 km. Turn left, and it is a short walk back to the parking lot and your car.

This hike has used 5.6 of the 8 km of trail at Susquehannock State Park, so your best bet for additional hiking would be at the Holtwood Recreation Area, to the north of PA 372 (see Hike 23).

18

Nolde Forest

Location: 2 miles south of Reading

Distance: 5.8 km (3.6 miles)

Time: 2½ hours

Vertical rise: 146 meters (480 feet)

Highlights: Evergreen plantations, stream

Maps: USGS 7½' Reading; park map

Jacob Nolde made his money in hosiery and, in the early 20th century, purchased 270 hectares of land on the hills south of Reading. At that time unproductive farmland covered the hills. Inspired by a single "pasture pine," Nolde hired an Austrian forester, William Kohout, and set about creating his own Black Forest with evergreen plantations of Douglas fir, Norway spruce, and Japanese larch, along with white, red, ponderosa, and Scotch pines. About 100,000 seedlings were planted per year for some 15 years. Mixed hardwoods—beech, oak, tulip, and red maple—also grow here now.

Nolde Forest was purchased by the state in the late 1960s, using Project 70 money; it was closed to hunting and turned into an environmental education center. On a given day, several school classes will be participating in environmental studies. Any break from the usual classroom routine must afford a painless path to learning. And the students think it's just a great field trip.

The trails along this hike are mostly old fire roads with an excellent footway, so walking shoes are fine for this hike. In fact, you could probably push a stroller on many of these trails. The hike is arranged as a figure 8; you could shorten it by walking only one of the loops.

How to Get There

Nolde Forest is located on PA 625, just 2 miles south of its junction with PA 724. Turn at the main entrance road and drive 0.5 mile to a parking lot near the mansion.

The main entrance is closed on weekends and holidays. Use the Sawmill entrance about 0.6 mile north on PA 625. Follow the gated paved road upstream to the junction with the Watershed Trail.

The Trail

Turn back down the entrance road and bear left on another road closed to traffic. This road descends into the valley of Punches Run. Turn left at a teaching station and bear left on the Watershed Trail. Look out for poison ivy. The trails at Nolde are not blazed, but there are signposts at many intersections. At 0.8 km turn left onto a road; bear right at the next junction. Jog left over a bridge at 1.1 km and continue up the Watershed Trail.

At 1.4 km the trail has relocated itself to get around a pile of blowdowns that have not been removed. Rejoin the old trail next to a springhouse. Pass among several smaller springhouses and turn right onto the Apple Tree Trail. (The park map is slightly in error at this point.) Then turn right onto the Spruce Trail, and left onto the Boulevard. Continue climbing gently to the top of the ridge.

In addition to the evergreen plantations, maple, oak, and tulip trees grow along your route. At 2.9 km there is a side trail to a rock outcrop; this hike swings right and continues on the Boulevard, which descends gently. At 3.6 km you reach a picnic area with rest rooms. The well here is no longer operational, but this is a good place for a lunch stop.

If you wish to truncate your hike, you can do so just beyond by turning left onto the Boulevard or the Watershed Trail and retracing your steps to your car. To continue this hike, though, turn right up the Cabin Hollow Trail. The trail climbs gently through a stand of hemlocks that appear to be dying from the woolly adelgid.

At the top of the hill, cross Laurel Path and continue on the Owl Trail through a stand of white pines. Along this section you may hear a flock of crows making a great fuss. They are probably "mobbing" an owl because they know what owls do to crows at night.

Cross Middle Road and, at 4.8 km, turn left onto Kissinger Road. At 5.5 km, just before Middle Road, turn right and continue downhill to the parking lot.

There are 10 km of trails at Nolde Forest not used by this hike. Additional hiking opportunities in the Reading area can also be found at Mill Creek (Hike 25) French Creek State Park, and to the east (Hike 30).

19

Ridley Creek

Location: 6 miles northwest of Media

Distance: 6.9 km (4.3 miles)

Time: 2½ hours

Vertical rise: 150 meters (490 feet)

Highlights: A pleasant walk in the woods

Maps: USGS 7½' Media; park map

Only 26 km from the center of Philadelphia is an oasis of peace and quiet. Except for an occasional jet or helicopter, the roar of traffic is absent and the silence is broken only by birdcalls. Ridley Creek is one of our newer state parks, purchased in the 1960s with Project 70 funds. Its 1,000 hectares contain more than 950 picnic tables; it sometimes gets really busy on a summer weekend. The park is gently rolling and occupies both banks of Ridley Creek. Some parts consist of fields reverting to woods, and others are mature timber.

Ridley Creek Park is closed to small-game hunting but does have a controlled deer hunt in-season. (Large areas of many Pennsylvania state parks are open to hunting.) The principal trail is a paved multiuse path forming an 8 km loop, which is used by walkers, joggers, and bicyclists. Horses are permitted in the northwest portion of the park. In addition, there are four conventional hiking trails—blazed white, yellow, blue, and red—on which bicycles are prohibited.

This hike is a circuit on the white trail. Walking shoes are adequate, except at the wettest times of the year.

How to Get There

The park can be reached from Gradyville Road; it is about 2.5 miles west of Newton Square. Or you can take PA 3 to either PA 352 or PA 252. Both these roads intersect Gradyville Road; from PA 352 you will drive east on Gradyville to reach the park, and from PA 252 you will drive west. The park can also be reached directly from PA 3 west of Newton Square via Sandy Flash Drive North.

To reach the trailhead for this hike, turn from Gradyville onto Sandy Flash Drive South and go 1.8 miles south. Pass the park office and follow signs to trailhead parking area 17.

The Trail

From parking area 17, make your way to the fitness court, then to the multiuse trail beyond. Turn left and walk 300 meters, then turn left again onto the white-blazed trail. There are no trail signs here, but many junctions are marked by posts banded with the appropriate color. Where two trails use the same path, both color blazes are used. Within a few steps the yellow-blazed trail turns left to area 17; you could use it to avoid the multiuse trail, if you prefer.

At 500 meters, the red-blazed trail joins from your left before turning off on its own. Next, you cross the yellow-marked trail and pass some large rocks. Just before you reach the multiuse trail, the blue-blazed trail comes in from your left. Turn right onto the multiuse trail for a short bit, then left onto the white-marked trail along Ridley Creek itself. Cross a side stream on a bridge and

continue up Ridley Creek. The trails all appear to be well maintained and are wide and easy to follow. In the mature forests you pass tulip, beech, ironwood, black gum, maple, and oak trees.

The trail then swings away from the creek and climbs to picnic area 9 at 2.6 km, which has rest rooms, picnic tables, and a parking lot. Walk out the access road. There are some white blazes on the pavement to direct you. Then turn left through a field that is revegetating with locust, crab apples, and multiflora roses.

Cross the yellow-blazed trail at the top of a ridge and descend, crossing a pipeline. Turn right on the multiuse trail and pass through a culvert under Sandy Flash Drive. Immediately beyond, turn left. Ahead is a confusing section where two white-blazed trails turn right. Keep left at both junctions. Continue past large tulip trees. On a bright day in fall, with the footway covered with colored leaves, this is an especially delightful trail.

At 4.2 km cross a stream and a road. Then climb over a hill and cross Sandy

Flash Drive at picnic area 16, with the usual facilities but only a couple of picnic tables. Beyond, the blue-blazed trail joins from your left; you cross the red-marked trail before the blue turns off to your right.

At 5.5 km, cross the road for the last time and continue through the woods on a sunken road. This is a particularly attractive section. Turn left up some steps and pass through a culvert under the multiuse trail. Turn left where the yellow-marked trail goes right (to the Tyler Arboretum). Next, you reach the multiuse trail. Turn left and return to parking area 17.

There are additional hiking opportunities at Ridley Creek on the yellow, blue, and red trails, as well as at the adjacent Tyler Arboretum (see Hike 28).

20

Skippack Creek Trail

Location: 6 miles north of Norristown

Distance: 7.5 km (4.7 miles)

Time: 2¾ hours

Vertical rise: 100 meters (320 feet)

Highlights: Creek

Maps: USGS 7½' Collegeville; park map

Evansburg State Park, in Montgomery County, the site of this hike, ought to be one of the 30 Best-Kept Secrets of Pennsylvania's State Parks. It is all but impossible to find, even with the park map in hand. I did not find any signs until we were in the park, and these said only STATE PARK—NO ROADSIDE PARKING. This is the most low-profile state park I've ever visited.

But Evansburg is worth the effort to find. It has Skippack Creek, a free-flowing stream; a loop trail; a youth hostel; more than 50 pre-Revolutionary structures; and the usual picnic area and equestrian trail. (Bicycles are prohibited on all hiking and equestrian trails.) Evansburg is an island of quiet on the fringes of Philadelphia.

The park was purchased as open space with Project 70 funds. The loop hiking trail was built by volunteers from a local chapter of the Appalachian Mountain Club. Many parks would be bereft of hiking trails were it not for volunteers.

How to Get There

Evansburg State Park can be reached from exit 31 off the Northeast Extension of the Pennsylvania Turnpike. Turn east onto PA 63. Where PA 63 turns left, continue straight ahead to a junction with PA 363. Turn right and drive 8.7 miles; then turn right onto Germantown Pike at a traffic light. After 2.7 more miles, and immediately beyond the Eight Arch Bridge over Skippack Creek, turn right. This is Skippack Creek Road. Follow it to Mill Road and continue into the park on May Hall Road. Park near the picnic pavilion.

You can also reach the park from PA 113 south of Skippack Village by driving east on Mill Road; and you can reach it from US 422 via PA 29 and Germantown Pike. There are also parking areas on Anders Road and Water Street that you could use as starting points.

The Trail

From the rest rooms at the picnic area, head toward the creek and turn left along the edge of the bank. Skippack Creek is at the bottom of the slope. The trail is marked with diamond-shaped dirty-white blazes. At 300 meters bear right downhill. The trail ahead goes to the nature center. Exhibits along the way show that you are on part of the Nature

Trail. One tells you about poison ivy, which is abundant in the park.

Cross the first of many footbridges. At 600 meters pass a junction with the Old Farmstead Trail. Cross another footbridge. The Horse Trail comes in from your left, and the two trails continue together for 100 meters until the footpath bears left. Then pass the Diehl House, vintage 1855, on your left.

The trail emerges briefly at the edge of a field but reenters the woods in 10 meters along the edge of Skippack Creek. Listen for the rattle of the kingfisher along the creek. As you cross a high-water cutoff of the creek, note the low cliffs on the far side at the foot of Hemlock Slope.

At 2.1 km pass the Isaac Cassel House, dating from 1771. Then climb the bank and bear right on an old road. Next, pass under a power line where the Horse Trail diverges to your left. Turn right onto Anders Road and cross Skippack Creek on the stone bridge. The bridge is closed to traffic, as parts of the upstream side are missing.

Now turn right on trail and pass under the power line again. Sycamore and beech trees grow along here. At 3.5 km turn left and climb Hemlock Slope, passing a new house to your left. Be careful on Hemlock Slope: You saw the cliffs from the other side of the creek. Then cross over the highest footbridge yet. Next, you come to a series of quarries that make the going a bit tougher. Note the poison ivy growing here.

Beyond Hemlock Slope you cross the Horse Trail twice, and then a couple of footbridges. At 5.5 km, continue ahead on paved Water Street Road. The trail bears right along the creek bank but has to return to the road to cross a bridge over a side stream.

Turn right and cross the Iron Bridge at 6.3 km. This bridge is also closed to traffic. Turn right on the far side and pass a house dating from 1753. Cross the millrace from Markley Hill, built in the 1750s, and continue above it.

Pass a large spruce and evergreen plantation to your left. After crossing a stream and another footbridge, you are back in the picnic area. Turn left to the parking lot.

21

Wissahickon Gorge

Location: North-central Philadelphia

Distance: 7.6 km (4.7 miles)

Time: 3 hours

Vertical rise: 140 meters (460 feet)

Highlights: Covered bridge

*Maps: USGS 7½' Germantown;
Wissahickon Valley Map*

Fairmount Park in Philadelphia, the site for this hike, is the largest municipal park of any city in the world. The southernmost portion contains the Philadelphia Museum of Art, with the famous *Rocky* steps. For hikers the best part is Wissahickon Gorge, in the northernmost part of the park. The gorge is about 10 km long and steep-sided, though of modest depth. In addition to the main gorge, there are side valleys that penetrate far into the surrounding city.

At one time the gorge was a center of industrial activity, due to the presence of waterpower. Many dams were built to power grist-, saw-, paper-, and textile mills. When the steam engine replaced waterpower in the middle of the 19th century, the city acquired the land.

There are a great many trails in Fairmount Park, most of them on old roads and grades. The mill owners lived on top of the gorge, and many of the roads were built for them to commute to work. Some of these trails are blazed, but others are not. Forbidden Drive (forbidden only to motor vehicles), mostly on the west side of Wissahickon Gorge, is an old carriage road along the creek itself. It is heavily used by joggers, dog walkers, bicyclists, horseback riders, and anglers. The eastern side of the gorge has more rugged trails on its steep slopes.

You will see on this hike that water is the enemy of trails. Some have been eroded to bedrock. The solution is to get water off the trails, and many water bars have been built of wood and stone by volunteers for this purpose. The volunteers wage a constant struggle to keep these water bars cleared and in good repair. If even a single rock is removed from a water bar, its usefulness is destroyed, because the water can then continue down the trail rather than being shunted off to the side. Perhaps some of these trails should be paved, and others closed.

This hike is a sample of the attractions of Wissahickon Gorge, but do not hike alone. Take a friend or a dog. The gorge has its share of urban problems.

How to Get There

Despite its size, Wissahickon Gorge is difficult to reach. There are only three park-

The Valley Green Inn

ing lots—one at the Valley Green Inn, another at Kitchen's Lane, and one on Bell's Mill Road—and they may be filled, even in midweek. This hike uses a different access point.

From exit 333 off the Pennsylvania Turnpike, follow Germantown Pike east. Keep right immediately after the tollbooths. Drive south into Philadelphia, about 4 miles. At the city limits, the pike becomes an avenue. One block after Bell's Mill Road, turn right onto Hampton Road, then left onto Crefeld Street. Crefeld swings left opposite house number 8917. The iron fence on your right looks like it belongs to a private estate but is actually the boundary of Fairmount Park. Park along the street.

Reaching this trailhead from elsewhere in the city may be more complicated. See any map of Philadelphia; there's one on the back of the official Pennsylvania road map.

The Trail

Near the far end of the iron fence there is a gate between two stone pillars. This is your entrance to the park. Please leave the gate closed. Bear right on a lavender-blazed trail that descends along an intermittent stream. After 300 meters, turn left onto an unblazed trail and cross a bridge over Crefeld Creek. Bear left, uphill, briefly on the lavender-marked trail, then turn sharply right onto an unblazed trail.

Next, turn right onto a white-blazed trail that comes in from Towanda Avenue. There is a stone wall opposite, along the edge of private land. After passing a bench, bear left downhill and turn left up some steps. At 1.6 km cross a bridge; beyond, there is a statue of a Native American crouching on a rock. The statue is said to represent Tedyuscung, a Lenni-Lenape chief (1720–63), but apparently the sculptor intended it to show a generic Native American.

Switchback downhill, then turn right onto an unblazed old road that leads to the Rex Avenue Bridge over the Wissahickon River. This stone bridge was built by the Works Progress Administration during the Great Depression. On the far side turn left onto Forbidden Drive and proceed downstream, passing a derelict storm shelter, then a dam. Bear left on a road open to automobiles. Pass a parking lot and reach the Valley Green Inn, the only surviving inn along the Wissahickon, at 3.9 km. Meals, maps, and rest rooms are available here. On raw days there may be a roaring fire inside to warm up by.

Then turn back upstream, passing the Rex Avenue Bridge to a covered bridge at 6.2 km. Cross it, and turn left onto an orange-blazed trail. Climb over rough trail, ignoring a steep trail that comes down from your right. Next, bear right onto an unblazed trail where the orange-blazed goes left to Bell's Mill Road. The unmarked trail swings right to Crefeld Creek, passing cascades and then joining the lavender-blazed trail. Continue climbing, briefly retracing your earlier route but this time sticking with the lavender-marked trail. Cross a stone bridge. A chain-link fence to your right marks the boundary of private land. Soon you are back at the gate to Crefeld Street.

There are plenty of additional hiking opportunities in Wissahickon Gorge. You may wish to become one of the volunteers who maintain these trails by joining Friends of the Wissahickon, Box 4068, Philadelphia, PA 19118. A map, "Roads, Paths, and Places of Interest in the Wissahickon Valley," is published by Friends of the Wissahickon; it can be obtained from them or from Way-to-Go (215-483-7387), 4363 Main Street, Philadelphia, PA 19127.

22

Valley Forge

*Location: Near the junction of I-76
and US 422 north of Philadelphia*

Distance: 7.8 km (4.9 miles)

Time: 3 hours

Vertical rise: 85 meters (280 feet)

Highlights: Historical site

*Maps: USGS 7½' Valley Forge;
park map*

Valley Forge is a shrine to our nationhood. It was here, in the winter of 1777–78, that the Revolution hit bottom for colonial forces. After a repulse at Germantown, the Continental army went into winter camp at Valley Forge. The site was both defensible and close enough to Philadelphia to keep an eye on the British there. Over the winter the force of 12,000 dwindled to 6,000 through death, desertion, and expired enlistments. (Of the 2,000 deaths, only one grave has been identified.) Rations and munitions were scarce to nonexistent. It looked like the end of the Revolution was near.

No battles were fought at Valley Forge. The British, snug in Philadelphia for the winter, never attacked. They didn't have to. His Majesty's troops dined well on food bought with British gold. Colonial soldiers could pay only in paper money "not worth a Continental." The colonial troops, weakened by near starvation (one soldier wrote that on some days his ration was 1 gill of rice, some days 2 ounces of meat, other days nothing) and the cold (many soldiers endured the winter with disintegrating clothes and no shoes or socks at all), fell prey to typhoid, typhus, dysentery, and smallpox.

And yet it was here, at Valley Forge, that the war turned around. The army that marched out in June 1778 had reached 20,000 and was better trained and equipped. Five more years of war lay ahead, but conditions were never again as bad as they were here. Covert aid from Spain and open recognition by France made the difference.

The emphasis in this park is on historical interpretation, not hiking, but there are still some opportunities for those who would rather see the park on foot than through a car window. It might seem that the ideal time for this hike would be April, when the redbud and dogwood are in bloom, but to really get a taste of the place you should come (without breakfast) on a bleak day in February.

How to Get There

Valley Forge can be reached from exit 326 off the Pennsylvania Turnpike. Follow signs 1.6 miles north and turn left for the Visitors Center. It can also be reached from US 422 and PA 23.

Stop in at the Visitors Center to see the exhibits and a short film. Most of this hike is on the paved Multi-use Trail, and walking shoes are preferable. Bicyclists and joggers are also permitted on the Multi-use Trail, so keep an eye out, particularly for the bicycles.

The Trail

This hike starts just beyond the auditorium and administration buildings. Head left and circle the Visitors Center. The trail continues along PA 23. In addition to dogwood and

A hut at Valley Forge

redbud, catalpa, sweet gum, and white pine grow here.

Cross County Line Road to a gentle climb. At 1.5 km pass a monument to patriots of African descent, then a side road to the site of General Huntingdon's quarters. Like most such buildings at Valley Forge, it is not open to the public.

At 1.9 km a path leads to the grave of a Lieutenant Waterman, the only identified grave of all the men who died that winter. Then you pass some reconstructed huts. They are dark and windowless, but sanitized—no dense, choking smoke issuing from the green wood burning in the chimneys, no groans or stench of men dying from "the bloody flux." More than 1,000 huts were built to shelter the Continental army that winter, but they were not completed in time for the army's arrival on December 19; it was mid-January before all the men could be housed. Next, pass the headquarters of General Varum. There seems to have been

no shortage of generals at Valley Forge. Today such a force would have only one.

Veer left to pass a statue of Friedrich von Steuben, a Prussian officer between jobs, not knowing a word of English but with a generous supply of German and French curses, who came to Valley Forge in late February 1778. Unlike American officers, he worked directly with the enlisted men. Von Steuben taught by example and intensively trained a special group of 100 men who then returned to their units to train the rest of the troops. Because many units were using different training manuals, he wrote a new, uniform manual for the whole army. More than any other man, Von Steuben is credited with turning a motley mix of soldiers into a disciplined fighting force at Valley Forge. The Grand Parade on which he trained his handpicked group is to your left.

Turn left, away from PA 23, and at 2.9 km turn left again onto the historic road trace.

Valley Forge

This road led north to a bridge over the Schuylkill River built that winter to bring in supplies. The road seems to have escaped much resurfacing since then.

Cross Gulph Road and bear left on the Multi-use Trail at 4 km. Next, turn left and circle Wayne's Woods to a picnic area with rest rooms. Continue past more huts, then circle the National Memorial Arch. (The arch is dilapidated and pieces of it keep falling off, so you can't go through it.) Soon, the Multi-use Trail parallels the Outer Line

Defenses at the top of a hill. Half a dozen brigades manned this line. Pass more huts and redoubt 2, which anchored the left flank of the Outer Line. Then cross two roads and complete your hike of Valley Forge at the administration building.

Additional hiking opportunities in the area can be found on Mount Joy, west of Valley Creek and north of the Schuylkill River. However, these trails are difficult to integrate with this hike because of bridge crossings and missing trail sections.

23

Holtwood Recreation Area

Location: 15 miles south of Lancaster

Distance: 8.1 km (5.0 miles)

Time: 3¼ hours

Vertical rise: 250 meters (820 feet)

Highlights: Conestoga Trail, view, stream

Maps: USGS 7½' Holtwood; recreation area map

The Holtwood Recreation Area, near the Maryland border, is owned by Pennsylvania Power and Light (PP&L) and was developed as part of the Holtwood Dam hydroelectric project when PP&L acquired tracts of land on both sides of the Susquehanna River. The Kelly's Run–Pinnacle Trail System is within this land on the river's east side.

PP&L has designated much of this site as Kelly's Run Natural Area, which means it will remain protected in its natural state. The Kelly's Run–Pinnacle Trail System has been designated a national recreation trail by the U.S. Department of the Interior.

As there is at least one stream crossing and a lot of rocks, you will want your boots for this hike.

How to Get There

The Holtwood Recreation Area is reached from PA 372. Turn north onto Crystal Drive, 1 mile east of the Norman Wood Bridge over the Susquehanna River. Then drive north 0.8 mile to the parking lot.

The Trail

Turn to your right and follow the edge of the woods until you see a post sign that says CONESTOGA TRAIL. Then head into the woods on a broad trail following blue (Kelly's Run Trail) and orange (Conestoga Trail) blazes. In a few steps you cross the yellow-blazed Oliver Patton Trail, named for the original farmer of this area.

The Conestoga Trail, built by the Lancaster Hiking Club, runs from the Horse

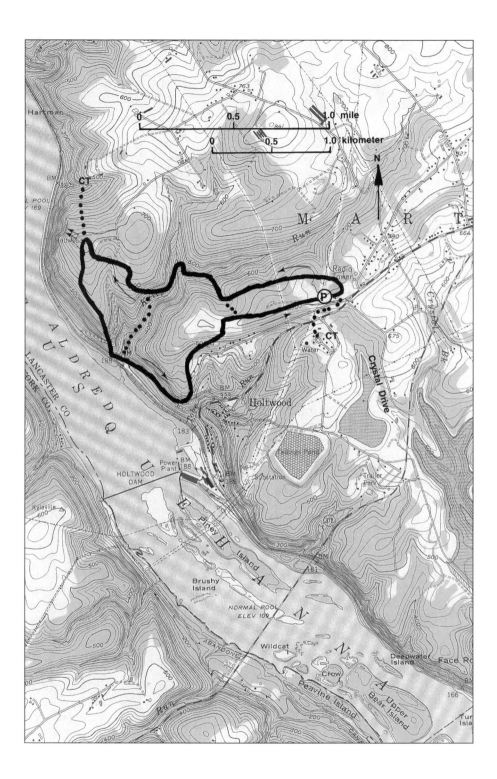

Shoe Trail crossing at US 322 to the Mason-Dixon Trail at the Lock 12 (Susquehanna and Tide Water Canal) historic area. It's about 105 km long. The best parts are from PA 372 north along the Susquehanna to Pequea and then east to Martic Forge.

Back on the Kelly's Run Trail, you soon pass under a power line. The Holtwood Dam supplies power at times of peak demand; transmission lines spread out in many directions. Next, cross the other side of the Oliver Patton Trail. Pass under another power line.

At a junction with the red-blazed Loop Trail on your left, the Kelly's Run Trail descends steeply to the run itself. (You could use the Loop Trail to truncate this hike by connecting with the Kelly's Run Return Trail.)

At 1.8 km there are cliffs of Wissahickon schist and the trail passes through rhododendrons. Cross Kelly's Run, then a side stream, and continue downstream.

Note that many of the hemlocks in this valley are dead or dying. This is due to the woolly adelgid, an aphid that sucks the juices from hemlock needles, weakening the trees. Some believe that hemlocks will go the way of the American chestnut at the turn of the last century, for the woolly adelgid has no natural enemies. *Tsuga canadensis* is Pennsylvania's state tree; it's scary to imagine our forests without these beauties.

At 2.4 km continue ahead on the white-blazed Pinnacle Trail. (You have another opportunity to shorten this hike by bearing left here on the Kelly's Run Trail.) Climb on the Pinnacle Trail and turn left, crossing first an old road, then a telephone cable swath. Turn right onto a fire road that is also blazed yellow.

Note an old stone wall as you climb: Somebody tried to farm this land. Pass a gate at the Pinnacle parking area and bear left to the overlook. There is a sweeping view across Lake Aldred and up to Otter Creek on the other side. Lake Aldred is formed by the Holtwood Dam. There are picnic tables and drinking water here in-season. "And when I asked the name of the river and heard it was called the Susquehanna; the beauty of the name seemed to be part and parcel of the beauty of the land . . ." –Robert Louis Stevenson.

To return, head back to the gate and bear right on the Fire Line Trail, blazed both yellow and orange. Soon you pass the other end of the stone wall you saw on your way up.

At 4.3 km bear right on the Conestoga Trail and descend, passing a lookout ledge to your right. Jog right 30 meters on the telephone cable swath, and continue in the woods. Next, turn right onto a woods road for 100 meters; then turn left onto rough trail that descends the rocky spine of the ridge.

Turn right onto the Kelly's Run Trail at 5 km, then left onto a paved road closed to traffic. Cross Kelly's Run on the road bridge and climb to a gate at the edge of a road open to traffic.

Turn left and left again, passing another gate. Climb on a grassy road to the edge of a field, where you turn left. Then turn right and cross the field on a track.

You will reach a junction with the other end of the red-blazed loop trail at 7.2 km. Cross a power line and pass a pine plantation. Cross another power line to arrive at the gate at the corner of the parking lot.

Additional hiking opportunities here include the Pine Tree Trail from the Pinnacle Overlook, and the Oliver Patton Trail. Or you could follow the Conestoga Trail north along the rugged river hills to Pequea or Martic Forge.

24

Tyler State Park

Location: Just west of Newtown

Distance: 8.7 km (5.4 miles)

Time: 2½ hours

Vertical rise: 110 meters (360 feet)

Highlights: A pleasant walk in the country

Maps: USGS 7½' Langhorne; park map

Tyler State Park in Bucks County (not to be confused with Tyler Arboretum in Delaware County) was purchased with Project 70 funds, then developed with funds from the Pennsylvania Land and Water Conservation and Recreation Act. There are a total of 38 km of trails in the park. Most are paved multiuse trails for bicyclists, walkers, joggers, hikers, and, in some places, equestrians. Neshaminy Creek divides the park into the eastern section, which is developed, and the western, where most of the trails are located. Since the Schofield Covered Bridge was destroyed by arson in 1991, the only link between east and west is a pedestrian causeway near the boathouse parking area.

Two low dams on Neshaminy Creek provide some slack water for boating. There is a youth hostel near the northern end of the park, and you may meet cars going to or from the hostel.

About 25 percent of the park is leased for agriculture; corn, winter wheat, hay, and soybeans are grown. After harvest, the cornfields are invaded by hundreds of Canada geese swooping down for fast food; some of the geese are permanent residents, but park officials hope that most are still migratory. There is no hunting at Tyler Park.

This hike is mostly on paved trails, so walking shoes are fine.

How to Get There

Tyler State Park is on PA 413 at its junction with Swamp Road. This part of PA 413 is the four-lane bypass just west of Newtown. The park can also be reached from exit 343 off the Pennsylvania Turnpike. Drive east on PA 332 from Willow Grove to Richboro, and continue to the park. PA 332 forms Tyler's southern boundary and intersects with PA 413 just east of the park.

There is a parking lot on No. 1 Lane (off PA 332) that you could use. This hike, however, uses the boathouse parking lot. From the main entrance on PA 413, follow Swamp Road for 0.4 mile to a stop sign. Turn right onto Main Park Road and drive 1.2 miles to the end, where you will find the boathouse parking lot.

The Trail

This circuit hike makes a grand tour of the western part of the park. Start by crossing the pedestrian causeway; the Neshaminy Weir Dam is just upstream. Then turn right onto the Mill Dairy Trail, passing tulip trees and white oaks. At 600 meters you walk by a historic farm building. In the park these houses are owned by the state but leased to private persons.

At 0.8 km turn right onto the Dairy Hill Trail. This and other major trail junctions are marked with signs. Red oak, shagbark hickory, sassafras, and hemlock trees can be seen along this trail. It returns to Neshaminy Creek, where you may hear the rattling call of the kingfisher. Note poison ivy vines climbing up trees along the trail. It's really a beautiful vine: The leaves turn red in the fall and it bears an abundance of white berries, eaten by birds.

At 2.5 km you reach a junction with the Covered Bridge Trail. There is a drinking fountain at this junction. Continue ahead on the White Pine Trail. (Yes, it really does have white pines.) Along the park boundary you pass a working farm.

Turn right at a junction with the Dairy Hill Trail at 3.3 km. The *Dairy* name figures in a number of trails because the Tylers, who owned this land before it became a park, operated a dairy farm here.

The Stone Bridge over Porter Run

Next, pass a junction with the Hay Barn Grass Trail and continue to the park boundary, passing private homes. Turn left onto the College Park Trail at 4.2 km. As usual, equestrian trails weave in and out of the hiker-biker trails.

Turn right onto the No. 1 Lane Trail and cross a stone bridge. At another historic house you reach the end of a road. Cross a bridge and turn left onto the Stable Mill Trail. As noted earlier, there is a parking lot ahead that can be reached from PA 332.

Pass the Gallery (Pennsylvania crafts), another parking lot, and a white stone house where the road is blocked to vehicles.

Osage orange is an abundant tree along this section. It produces bright green fruits that look like warty oranges but are of a very different consistency.

At 6.4 km there is a junction with the Natural Area Trail, which is different from the Nature Trail along Porter Run. Turn left onto the Mill Dairy Trail at 7.3 km, cross a bridge, and bear right on the Woodfield Trail. This is a fitness trail, but the exercises are optional.

Turn right onto the Mill Dairy Trail again, walking among some beech trees. Pass the other end of the Natural Area Trail. Cross a stone bridge over Porter Run, turn right, cross the pedestrian causeway, and return to your car.

25

Mill Creek

Location: 10 miles southeast of Reading

Distance: 10.9 km (6.8 miles)

Time: 4 hours

Vertical rise: 320 meters (1,050 feet)

Highlights: Large rocks, creek

Maps: USGS 7½' Elverson, Pottstown; park map

This hike explores the roadless eastern section of French Creek State Park. For more than a century the Hopewell Iron Furnace produced iron from local ores and charcoal. The charcoal was itself produced from trees growing on the hills around French Creek. These hills were repeatedly denuded of trees, marginalizing the land. Then, during the Great Depression of the 1930s, the lands were purchased by the federal government. Today's forest shows how well the hills have recovered.

There are rocks and a lot of wet areas along the trail, so wear your hiking boots. Most of the trails open to mountain bikes are on this side of PA 345 and are maintained by mountain bikers. The trails are still open to hikers, but try to stay out of bikers' way; they may feel possessive. The Lenape and part of the Raccoon Trails on this hike stray onto land belonging to the Hopewell Furnace National Historic Site. Hopewell now charges user fees on individuals, so technically you are liable for this fee, but it is unlikely that Hopwell will station anybody on these trails to collect fees. Alternatively, you may choose to return on the Mill Creek Trail and thus avoid any fee. See the park map.

How to Get There

French Creek State Park can be reached from exit 298 off the Pennsylvania Turnpike: Follow PA 10 to Morgantown, then take PA 23 east to PA 345. The park is also accessible from exit 312: Follow PA 100 north to PA 23, then drive west on PA 23 to PA 345.

The trailhead is on PA 345 at its junction with Shed Road. This spot is 4.8 miles north of the junction with PA 23 and just 0.2 mile north of the east entrance to the park. Leave your car in a small area on your right, just beyond Shed Road. There is no sign at the trailhead.

The Trail

Cross Shed Road and head into the woods on the Mill Creek Trail, whose blazes are white with a red stripe across the middle. There are also green blazes here for the Lenape Trail, which also follows this part of the Mill Creek Trail.

Soon you bear right on a gated old road and climb gently. At 0.5 km continue straight ahead on the Mill Creek Trail where the Lenape Trail diverges to your right. (You will return on the Lenape Trail.) Cross a power line and reach a junction where the Mill Creek Trail splits. Turn left onto the trail and descend gently, passing a charcoal pit,

to Millers Point at 2.9 km. Millers Point is a large rock formation. It is easily climbed, but there is no view. White oak, maple, and sassafras grow on the uplands.

In-season the ground hereabouts is covered with mayapples. Stay on the Mill Creek Trail as it turns right and descends, passing a spring. Then turn left at a junction with a blue-and-red-blazed trail. (You could truncate your hike by turning right at this junction.)

Continue descending to 3.5 km, where you turn right. There are some good-sized tulip trees here in Mill Creek Valley.

This section of the trail has some old white blazes in addition to the white ones with the red stripe. At 4.2 km cross the first part of Mill Creek. The trail continues among large boulders. Just after a junction with the red-blazed Raccoon Trail (which could be used to shorten this hike), cross the main part of Mill Creek.

Then turn sharply right at 4.6 km and climb gently on an old eroded road. (To your left, this old road leads out to Sycamore Road.) At 5.4 km, where the old road continues ahead, turn right on trail.

In-season you can find spring beauties and jack-in-the-pulpits along the trails. Cross the headwaters of Mill Creek and climb gently. Beech trees and black birches grow along this section.

After you reach the top of the hill, turn right onto the Mill Creek Trail at a junction with the red-and-yellow-blazed Buzzards Trail. (You could extend this hike by following the Buzzards Trail into the southeast part of French Creek Park.) Next, the red-blazed Raccoon Trail comes in from your right and merges with the Mill Creek Trail.

At 7.2 km turn left onto the Raccoon Trail to vary your return. It is closed to bikes on this side of Mill Creek Trail. Follow it downhill, reaching the boundary of the Hopewell Furnace National Historic Site. At 8 km an unblazed trail comes in from your left, past the ruins of a stone building. Cross under the power line again.

Turn right onto the green-blazed Lenape Trail at 8.5 km. You will come to a bridge over a small stream. To your right, a short unblazed trail leads to a spring that bubbles up out of the rocks; to your left you can see a field through the trees, with Williams Hill beyond. Continue on, passing a springhouse to your left and climbing steps made from creosoted utility poles. A century ago such springs provided settlers with much of their best water. Now they are all polluted.

The Lenape Trail switchbacks up the hill to 10.4 km, where you bear left again on the Mill Creek Trail. Retrace your steps to your car on PA 345.

French Creek State Park has nearly 50 km of trails. This hike—together withFrench Creek State Park (Hike 30)—uses only 30 of them, so there are plenty of additional hiking opportunities at French Creek.

26

White Clay Creek

Location: At the junction of Pennsylvania, Delaware, and Maryland

Distance: 13.6 km (8.5 miles)

Time: 4¾ hours

Vertical rise: 50 meters (160 feet)

Highlights: Stream, quietness

Maps: USGS 7½' West Grove, Newark West DE-MD-PA; park map

White Clay Preserve in Pennsylvania and the state park of the same name in Delaware protect the valley of White Clay Creek. In the 1960s the valley was threatened with construction of a dam that would have flooded it. Under the leadership of Dorothy Miller and helped by a 688-hectare donation from the Du Pont family, the valley was preserved on both sides of the border. The dam project was not abandoned until the 1980s.

The Pennsylvania portion is designated as a preserve, the only one in the state park system, which means it doesn't have ball fields or picnic areas, but it does have a nature center near the London Tract Meeting House. The state park in Delaware has more amenities—but it also has user fees based on cars. If you are going to park in Delaware, it will cost five dollars if you are out-of-state. This hike is written so that you park in Pennsylvania. Don't get me wrong: I think user fees are the wave of the future, but if they can be evaded by walking across the border, why not? Beavers have been reintroduced into the valley and appear to be thriving. You will see evidence of their work along the trail: a pile of sticks, a gnawed-down tree stump, or even a freshly chewed branch across the trail. Will they succeed in damming White Clay Creek where human engineers failed?

How to Get There

The trailhead is parking lot 1 on London Tract Road in the northern part of the pre-

To PA 41

Quarry

Broad Run

North Bank Sch.

D O N   B R I T A I N

London Tract Rd.

Creek

WHITE CLAY CREEK

STATE PRESERVE

Creek

PENNSYLVANIA - CHESTER CO.
DELAWARE - NEW CASTLE CO.

WHITE CLAY CR.
STATE PK.

London Tract Cem.

ROAD

ROAD

Footbridge

WHITE CLAY CREEK
STATE PRESERVE

CHESTER CO.
NEW CASTLE CO.

STATE   PRESERVE

B R I T A I N

White   Clay   Creek

WHITE

SOUTH

Thompson

Unami
Trail

26. White Clay Creek

P Parking

N

0   1/2 mile

0   1/2 kilometer

PENNSYLVANIA
DELAWARE

OLD R.R. GRADE   ROAD

WHITE CLAY CREEK
STATE PRESERVE

serve. It can be reached from PA 896 by turning onto Indiantown Road across from London Britain Mall. Cross Flint Hall Road and turn left onto Glen Road after 0.8 mile. Continue ahead at the junction with London Tract Road at 1.7 miles. The parking lot is on your right 3 miles from PA 896. This trailhead can also be reached from PA 41 by turning south onto Newark Road, right onto Buttonwood Road, and then right again onto Broad Run Road, crossing White Clay Creek. Bear left on London Tract Road to parking lot 1.

The Trail

Cross the bridge at the corner of the parking lot and turn right onto the grade of the long-abandoned Newark & Pomeroy Railroad. Occasional blue blazes show that the Penndel Trail is part of the Mason-Dixon Trail—a wide-ranging path linking the Appalachian Trail on South Mountain with the Brandywine Trail via Maryland and Delaware. Part of this hike, particularly the gated Peltier Road, is open to horses and bicycles as well as hikers. However, the only piles of horse evidence I saw were on a section of the Penndel open only to hikers.

The bottomlands have produced many large trees: sycamore, tulip, pin oak, and hickory. The Newark & Pomeroy Railroad was built in the 1870s, but failed in the Great Depression. The steel was pulled in World War II for scrap. The trail soon passes a marsh on your right with a viewpoint opposite a bench.

At 800 meters the trail bears left off the railroad grade, passing box elder, ironwood, and dogwood trees. Off the trail, the bottomland is a jungle so filled with multiflora rose that you won't even notice the poison ivy—until later. Next, pass a concrete bridge abutment and piers where the Newark & Pomeroy crossed White Clay Creek.

At 1.5 km you pass the 1-mile marker—a tad short, but perhaps it was measured from the London Tract Road crossing, not the parking lot. Passing a cornfield to your left, you'll find that the trail is back on the Newark & Pomeroy grade, but almost at once you bear right off this grade, with the bridge piers of another crossing visible to your left. The trail continues along the base of a slope and then turns right along the middle branch of White Clay Creek.

At 2.7 km, turn left onto Sharpless Roadcross a steel bridge over the Middle Branch, and then turn left on trail. Soon you pass the horse ford across White Clay Creek and then the remains of Yeatman Station Road. Parking lot 2 is to your right. Next, pass the 2-mile marker, cross a couple of wooden bridges, and turn left onto Peltier Road. Peltier Road is open to horse and bicycle traffic, but is wider than Penndel Trail and has a gravel base. (The London Tract Meeting House and nature center are most easily reached by turning right at this junction and then turning right again onto South Bank Road.)

Pass the 3-mile marker at 4.8 km, then turn left at the Delaware boundary. (At this point the Mason-Dixon "line" is actually the arc of a large circle.) The trail follows closely along White Clay Creek, and more bridge ruins can be seen from a bench. Then climb to the railroad grade and follow it for 100 meters before bearing left and continuing along the edge of a large open field to your right.

At 5.8 km reach a fee parking lot and picnic tables on Chambers Rock Road. Cross Chambers Rock Road on the white-painted zebra and continue on trail along White Clay Creek to a junction with Peltier Road at 7.1 km. The nature center is just ahead in the old Chambers House, but rest rooms are immediately to your left. The center is open much of the year.

Beaver workings

To return a different way, turn uphill on Peltier Road and climb, passing a vehicle gate and walking along the edge of a field. Cross Chambers Rock Road at 8.1 km and continue through woods to the Mason-Dixon line (Pennsylvania border) at 8.8 km. Continue on the Peltier Road and retrace your steps to parking lot 1 and your car.

Most of the additional hiking opportunities at White Clay Creek are on the Delaware side of the line. Still, in Pennsylvania you can hike to the arc corner where the Mason-Dixon line and circle meet, and also to the tristate marker. See the park map.

27

The Pinnacle

Location: 3 miles northeast of Hamburg

Distance: 14.0 km (8.7 miles)

Time: 5 hours

Vertical rise: 315 meters (1,030 feet)

Highlights: Views, mountain stream

Map: USGS 7½' Hamburg; KTA sections 1–6

The Pinnacle is the most famous view on the Appalachian Trail in Pennsylvania, and one of the best in the state. A view from the Pinnacle is on the cover of *Pennsylvania Hiking Trails,* 11th edition. This trail's usage level is comparable to that of Hawk Falls (Hike 31), making it one of the most heavily traveled in the state.

This hike has more than its fair share of rocks, so wear your hiking boots.

How to Get There

Take exit 30 off I-78 at Hamburg. Follow Fourth Street south to a Uni-Mart and Getty station. Turn sharply right onto Port Clinton Avenue and proceed for 0.6 mile, passing under I-78. Turn right onto Mountain Avenue at a sign for Blue Mountain Camp. Drive 2.8 miles (the road name changes to Mountain Road) and turn left onto Reservoir Road. In 0.4 mile you reach the parking area, just before a chain-link fence at the Hamburg Reservoir. No overnight parking is permitted here.

The Trail

At the trailhead, a large NO TRESPASSING sign proclaims the entire water company area off-limits. Actually, the company is far more generous and does permit day hiking. Please read the posted regulations and abide by them so that this happy situation will continue.

If the gate to the fenced-off area is open, you can walk right through and pick up the blue blazes beyond the mapboard. If the gate is closed, use a well-beaten path immediately to the left of the fence.

Proceed up the blue-blazed gravel road to a junction with the white-blazed Appalachian Trail (AT). Turn right and cross a bridge over Furnace Run; then bear right again.

At 1.3 km turn right onto another old road at a trail junction. (The blue-blazed side trail leads ahead to the Windsor Furnace Shelter.) The old road climbs gently, passing chestnut oak and sassafras trees, in addition to American chestnuts. Along this hike, note the many American chestnuts that continue to sprout from old roots, even after the chestnut blight killed the mature trees.

The serious climb starts at 2.5 km. At 3 km a blue-blazed side trail goes right to the Blue Rocks Campground. Stay on the old road until 3.5 km, where you turn right onto a rough trail with stone steps. The first of many patches of poison ivy is found here.

At 3.8 km you reach Pulpit Rock, with views to the east and south. A river of rocks, called Blue Rocks, is visible below. These views are just a sneak preview of those from the Pinnacle. Note the astronomical observatory to your left. It is

---

The Pinnacle

The view from the Pinnacle

difficult for even the smallest observatories to avoid light pollution, even in rural areas. In a city you can't see even the brightest stars.

Follow the AT past an antenna site along the rocky edge of the ridge. At one point the trail passes through a crevasse. At 6.7 km there is a junction with a yellow-blazed trail on your right that also leads to the Blue Rocks Campground. Stay on the AT, which continues to be rough, rocky, and slow going.

At 7.3 km you reach a junction with a blue-blazed trail to your right that leads to the Pinnacle in 130 meters. Take this trail—but be careful, as there is a quite adequate drop to the rocks below. Views sweep east along heavily wooded Blue Mountain and then around to the south over farms, small towns, isolated hills, and the Cumberland Valley (the Great Valley of the Appalachians) to Furnace Hills on the horizon. Take your time savoring these views, but avoid the luxuriant poison ivy that grows here. The

Blue Mountain Eagle Climbing Club maintains a trail register here.

When the flight of time urges you, return to the junction with the AT and keep right. The trail continues to be rocky until 8 km, where you reach the end of a jeep road. The AT follows this road past a couple of small ponds. Hemlocks and black gum trees grow here. Proceed to a large grassy area at 10.3 km, known as the heliport.

Turn sharply left onto another jeep road partway across this clearing. This road makes for very easy hiking and you descend gently, passing a spring, then crossing Furnace Creek. (This is not Gold Spring, which is farther along and closer to the AT.) Black birch trees grow along the road, and the run has the expected stand of hemlocks.

There are a few blue blazes along the jeep road, but you don't really need them to find your way. Farther along, rhododendrons line the stream. This trail is quite a contrast to the AT between Pulpit Rocks and the Pinnacle.

At 12.4 km you reach the Hamburg Reservoir itself. Keep left, passing the dam. Continue ahead, ignoring a road to your left. At a junction with the AT, you close your loop by turning right, crossing Furnace Run, then turning left onto the blue-blazed road back to your car.

You could extend this hike about 1.5 km by following the AT "north" (toward Maine) to a woods road that descends Blue Mountain west of the reservoir. This route avoids Furnace Creek, however.

28

Wilderness Trail

Location: 4 miles northwest of Media

Distance: 14.1 km (8.7 miles)

Time: 5½ hours

Vertical rise: 245 meters (800 feet)

Highlights: Tyler Arboretum

Maps: USGS 7½' Media; visitors guide

The plantings at the Tyler Arboretum were begun by Minshall and Jacob Painter, who set aside part of their land for the systematic planting of trees and shrubs. Only about 20 of the original trees planted in the mid–19th century survive, but they are of real size. Among these original Painter trees are a cedar of Lebanon that is more than 4.5 meters in circumference and a giant, vintage-1856 sequoia. Even if you come back in 800 years, though, this one won't look like sequoias in the Sierras: This specimen has two trunks because a Christmas tree thief cut off its top in 1895.

This hike takes you on a grand tour of the 260-hectare arboretum. It is difficult to squeeze this long a trail into such a small area, so it has been folded and refolded to increase its length. There are seven blazed trails at Tyler, ranging in length from 2 km (the Dogwood and Pinetum Trails) on up to the 13.6 km Wilderness Trail. In addition to the blazed trails at Tyler, there are a host of unblazed trails and old roads. Admission to this private, not-for-profit educational institution is five dollars per person. Spring, when the shrubs and wildflowers are in bloom, is the best time to visit.

How to Get There

The Tyler Arboretum is located just off PA 352 about 4 miles north of Media; or you can take PA 352 south from PA 3 for 5.1 miles. In either case, turn east onto Forge Road, then right onto Painter Road to the parking lot.

The Trail

From the bulletin board at the corner of the parking lot, make your way toward the barn that houses the bookstore and rest rooms. Keep to the left of the building and descend a flight of steps to the cedar of Lebanon. Avoid the branch that touches the ground and continue to a bridge over Rocky Run, which serves as the trailhead.

The Wilderness Trail is blazed white. The sign at the loop junction indicates that these blazes are square, but they are in fact frequently rectangular and on their sides. Ignore all other-colored blazes. At the sign for the Wilderness Trail, take the left fork.

Along the way you will see azalea, rhododendron, dogwood, and lots of tulip tree. On the other hand, there is remarkably little poison ivy at Tyler. Turn right just beyond a fence at 1.2 km; a field to your left contains a dogwood. At 1.5 km turn left. A field of dogwood is to your right.

Cross Rocky Run at 2.2 km, then turn left and climb. Rocky Run has an abundance of skunk cabbage. Turn right, along the boundary between Ridley Creek Park and the Tyler Arboretum, at 2.6 km. There is a white pine plantation on the park side of the trail. Pass a trail leading into the state park.

At 3 km bear right, away from the boundary, on a recent relocation. Jog left at the next junction. At 3.3 km the trail has recently been hacked through the brush. Just beyond there is a bridge over a stream; turn right onto an old road and climb.

Wilderness Trail

There is an inviting bench at 3.7 km. Next, descend and turn sharply left above Rocky Run. Turn right at 4 km, at a corner marked with double arrows as well as double blazes, and recross Rocky Run on stepping-stones. Climb the hill and, at 4.9 km, turn left where a field of dogwood lies ahead. Then turn left again at the corner of another field. There are ruins to the left of the trail at 5.4 km; turn sharply left and pass below them.

Cross a bridge over Dismal Run and pass through a small fish hatchery. Note that the road here is on top of an old dam. At the far side of the valley, cross an old mill-race. At 5.8 km turn left off the road and pass through the floodplain of Dismal Run. Then turn left onto an old road and climb to Barren Road at 6.4 km. Cross with care and enter the east woods.

There is much less of a footway here, and you must move carefully from blaze to blaze. At 7.3 km the trail returns to Barren Road before turning sharply left. There is a woodlot management trail along this section.

Cross Barren Road again at 8.9 km, then turn left at a confusing spot (the arrow is intended for hikers going in the opposite direction). The trail reclimbs the hill before turning right near the junction of Painter and Barren Roads. At 9.9 km there is another confusing spot, where the white blazes bear to the right, then return to the old road. You could follow the blazes at this point, or just go straight ahead.

At 10.1 km cross Painter Road, then a stream, and climb to the edge of a field. Continue along the upper edge of this field, passing a bench under a cedar tree. The trail returns to Barren Road before turning right. Houses can be seen on adjacent private land along this section.

Cross Dismal Run on a log at 11.4 km. In high water, this could be interesting. Then turn left and proceed to 11.6 km, where you turn right. At 12 km pass another ruin with two keystone arches; turn right again. Cross Painter Road for a second time at 12.5 km. At 12.7 km turn right along the edge of an open area. Turn left into this open area at 12.8 km. Follow the blazes carefully, as there are very few of them. Turn left again at 13 km and follow trail past larches, then past the giant sequoia. Reenter the woods at 13.4 km and turn left among rhododendrons. Close the loop at 13.8 km, cross the bridge over Rocky Run, and retrace your steps to the parking lot.

There are six other blazed trails at Tyler but you have already covered many sections of them on the Wilderness Trail. There are also hiking opportunities at nearby Ridley Creek State Park; see Hike 19.

29

Delaware Canal

Location: 10 miles south of Easton

Distance: 17.3 km (10.8 miles)

Time: 4½ hours

Vertical rise: 15 meters (50 feet)

Highlights: National Heritage Trail

Maps: USGS 7½' Riegelsville, Frenchtown (NJ); park map

Following the success of the Erie Canal in 1825, Pennsylvania pursued a canal-building program in order to keep up with New York State. The Delaware Canal, 96 km long, was opened in 1832. Boats hauled coal, lumber, iron, and stone downriver, but they had trouble finding heavy cargoes for the return journey. Moving night and day, a canal boat took 2 days to traverse the canal from Easton to tidewater at Bristol, for an average of 2 km per hour. This is about half the rate at which you can walk the towpath.

Canals contained the seeds of their own destruction. First, they could operate only during the ice-free months. Trains had no such limitation. Second, canals had to be built along rivers to get the water they required. Rivers flood, and when they do they can damage or destroy a canal. Finally, canals were the first large-scale engineering projects in this country, and they trained a generation of engineers—who went on to build railroads.

Despite the odds against it, the Delaware Canal continued to operate until 1932. Thus, it survived more or less intact. Almost all of it still contains water, but the locks don't work anymore. The canal became a state park in 1940.

This is a long but easy (easy to follow and easy on your feet) hike on the canal's towpath. There is scarcely any change in elevation, and the footway is mowed grass and dirt. Save for the occasional tree root, you don't have to watch every step; you can look around. But do not stray off the towpath onto private land. Relations with adja-

The towpath and canal

cent owners are generally good; let's keep it that way. None of the park is open to hunting, but some may occur on private lands near the canal.

How to Get There

The linear structure of the canal dictates a car-shuttle hike. The canal is paralleled by PA 32 and PA 611. The northern end of this hike is at Lock 21, which is 1.8 miles north of Kintnersville, at the junction of PA 212 with PA 611. Parking places along the canal are hard to find, but there are a modest number here. Leave one car here and head south on PA 611. In Kintnersville turn left onto PA 32 and drive 9.4 miles to Tinicum County Park. Turn right and make your way to the edge of the canal, about 0.4 mile, where there is a small parking lot.

The Trail

Head north along the canal. This particularly attractive section follows the base of the hills; the highway is some distance away. At 900 meters you pass several houses. Many people live right on the canal. Some of the houses are definitely upscale, but there are also trailer camps.

The first bridge you reach is the only covered bridge on the canal. It is at 2.2 km, just before Lock 18. There are a lot of other bridges over the canal: I counted 19, including the one at Lock 21.

There are a great many different trees along the canal. I found maple, osage orange, pin oak, catalpa, white pine, sycamore, locust, willow, and river birch. Trees that grow next to the towpath enjoy an abundance of water and may achieve impressive size.

On this hike I've also seen great blue herons, kingfishers, juncos, titmice, chickadees, and a broad-winged hawk. Bluebird houses at some spots mean that in summer you should look for this bird that carries the sky on its back. Along the more isolated sections of the towpath you may find deer and raccoon tracks in the mud.

In some places the hills on the far side of the canal become real cliffs. At 5.2 km you reach Lock 19 and the Delaware Canal State Park headquarters. There is intermediate parking at Lock 19. On occasion there are mileposts along the towpath, but many seem to be missing.

You will find the Country Store at 7.6 km. Here you can obtain deli sandwiches and baked goods, and there is a rest room for customers. Beyond, the Delaware River becomes visible briefly. At 8.5 km PA 32 goes over the canal on a bridge next to the Manor House, an upscale restaurant.

At 11.5 km you can see PA 32 on one side, the Delaware on the other. Next, you pass the Indian Rock Inn. The cliffs tower in this area, and some people think they see the profile of a Native American in them. Don't spend too much time looking for it.

At 12.7 km you pass the Gilbert generating plant on the New Jersey side of the river. Next, you come to Lock 20, which has some picnic tables and is alleged to have some parking along the highway.

After a riffle in the Delaware, you will cross—at 13.9 km—Gallows Run aqueduct. Traugers Farm Market is at 15.7 km. PA 611 is now on the other side of the canal. Finally, you reach Lock 21 and your car.

There is additional hiking along the canal both north and south of this section, but finding parking places is a problem. To the north there is parking at Locks 22 and 23, Wy-Hit-Tuk County Park, and the Hugh Moore Park and Canal Museum in Easton. (After your hike, this museum is worth a visit.) To the south there is parking at Erwinna, the Mountain Side Inn (abandoned) south of Point Pleasant, Lumberville (a pulloff), the Virginia Forest Recreation Area, New Hope (on the street), Chez Oddets (park property) south of New Hope, Bowmans Hill in Washington Crossing Historical Park (one-dollar fee), the junction of PA 532, and Yardley (on Black Road).

30

French Creek State Park

Location: 11 miles southeast of Reading

Distance: 18.5 km (11.5 miles)

Time: 6½ hours

Vertical rise: 353 meters (1,160 feet)

Highlights: Horse Shoe Trail

Maps: USGS 7½' Elverson; park map

French Creek (2,900 hectares), between Reading and Philadelphia, is one of the large state parks that were operated as demonstration national parks by the federal government during the Great Depression. Recreational facilities such as dams, roads, picnic areas, group camps, and tent camping areas were built by the Civilian Conservation Corps (CCC). Those who loved Franklin Roosevelt said that the CCC was the best thing he did for the country. Those who hated him said the CCC was the only good thing he did. Even today, many of our recreation areas stem from the CCC.

The program also saved a generation of young men from becoming homeless drifters when they finished school only to find no jobs available. The CCC offered a little money and hearty meals to young men, physical work in the out-of-doors, and military discipline. The 3 million who were trained under this system became a large, albeit unorganized, reserve. More than 85 percent of the men who had been in the CCC served in World War II; in December 1941, many camps marched straight off to war.

The federal government bought up marginal areas such as French Creek during the Great Depression, giving the impoverished residents enough money to start over somewhere else with better chances. The land around French Creek had been logged repeatedly to make charcoal for the Hopewell Iron Furnace, which operated from 1771 to 1883. (Hopewell iron was used to make cannons during the Revolution.) In 1946 the park was turned over to the state, with the exception of a core area that the National Park Service retained as Hopewell Furnace National Historic Site.

This boot-busting hike makes a grand tour of the western part of the park. It is long, but you will have many opportunities to truncate it via other trails and roads. Given the many rocks and wet places, as well as the length of this hike, wear your boots.

How to Get There

French Creek can be reached from exit 298 off the Pennsylvania Turnpike. At the second traffic light in Morgantown, turn east onto PA 23 through Elverson. Then turn north onto PA 345 at Warwick. After 2.5 miles turn left into the park at its south entrance. After 1.1 miles turn right onto Park Road at a stop sign. Proceed 0.5 mile past the park office to the Hopewell Lake Boat Launch parking lot.

The park can also be reached from the north by following PA 345 south from just east of Birdsboro. Turn right on Park Road and proceed west to the Hopewell Lake Boat Launch.

The Trail

To start the hike, make your way to the left-hand corner of the parking lot, turn left, pass between the posts of a vehicle barrier, cross a bridge over an inlet to the lake, and pick up the blue-blazed Boone Trail. Bear left and briefly follow a paved road. Circle the swimming pool and pass through a picnic area, following the shore of Hopewell Lake. At the corner of the dam, turn left onto the yellow-blazed Horseshoe Trail (HST). The HST is almost unique in the East, as it was built for both equestrians and hikers. It crosses private land that is undergoing intense development; this has led to its listing by the Keystone Trails Association as one of four endangered hiking trails in Pennsylvania. Some trails at French Creek are still multiuse. Horses are permitted on the HST and on the right berm of most public roads. Mountain bikes are permitted on roads and approved trails only, and all trails south of Park Road are closed to mountain bikes.

Pass below the dam and cross the outlet. At the far end of the dam continue on the blue-blazed Boone Trail, which follows along paved Park Road. Then turn right and cross Park Road at 2.7 km. Climb on the Boone Trail, crossing the road to the campground. Turn left onto the green-blazed Lenape Trail at 3.3 km and follow the edge of the campground. The Lenape and Boone Trails turn left along the west side of the campground, but you continue ahead on a nameless trail marked orange with a green stripe across the middle.

To the north of the campground, turn right onto the orange-blazed Six Penny Trail, leaving the campground behind. Cross an unpaved road and turn left, then descend Brush Hill. The trail has mostly been relocated to keep it out of the eroded old charcoal road. Partway down you pass a charcoal hearth to your left.

Turn left at 6.6 km, still following the Six Penny Trail away from PA 345 and its noisy traffic. The trail passes scattered giant mountain laurels. Pass a junction with the purple-blazed Kalmia Trail. Next, pass a meadow at the Six Penny area that used to be a lake but was drained years ago. The charred ruins of the changing stockade can still be seen among the woods. Pass a spring and, at 8.5 km, turn left onto the yellow-blazed HST. Climb, passing the other end of the Kalmia Trail on your left and private land on your right and then the other end of Six Penny Trail on your left. Turn right onto the HST where the Boone Trail comes in and follow it downhill, circling the group tenting area. Then turn left and cross Scotts Run Road at 9.8 km. Continue through a picnic area, then cross Scotts Run below the dam forming Scotts Run Lake. The HST proceeds west, passing a junction with the Boone Trail on your right.

The Boone Trail turns left at 11.8 km; you continue on the HST to a crossing of paved Fire Tower Road at 12.0 km. It is gated off to traffic, but there is trailhead parking just beyond the gate to your right.

Continue on the white-blazed Turtle Trail and HST, which circle the base of Williams Hill, passing so close to the park boundary that you can see several houses on the adjacent private land. Pass a junction with red-blazed Ridge Trail at 13.8 km and then an unmarked trail that leads right to Cold Run Road. Continue past a white-blazed trail and then pick up the blue-blazed Boone Trail. Turn right onto the Boone Trail at 17.8 km and follow it across Park Road to the boat-launch parking lot on Hopewell Lake, where you left your car.

There is an abundance of additional hiking at French Creek. Mill Creek (Hike 25) explores the less developed section of the park east of PA 345.

IV

The Poconos

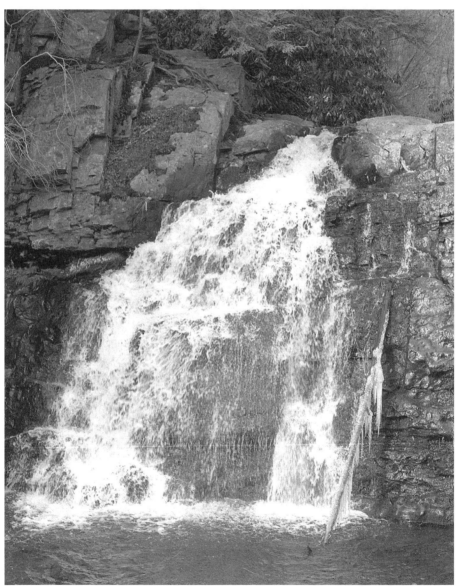

Hawk Falls

31

Hawk Falls

*Location: Hickory Run State Park,
near the junction of I-80 and I-476*

Distance: 4.8 km (3.0 miles)

Time: 2¼ hours

Vertical rise: 135 meters (440 feet)

Highlights: Cascades and waterfalls

*Maps: USGS 7½' Blakesley,
Hickory Run; park map*

Hickory Run State Park, at the western edge of the Poconos, is the setting for this short circuit hike. The Orchard Trail along Mud Run has recently been cleared and re-blazed yellow, making it a delight to follow. Despite its name, Mud Run is a beautifully clear stream attracting trout anglers (fly-fishing only) and kayakers (lots of drops). Mud Run flows through banks of rhododen-drons on its way to the Lehigh River. In ad-dition, there is a bridgeless crossing of Hawk Run. When the water level is high enough for the falls to be impressive, the crossing gets interesting. There are step-ping-stones, but they may be under water.

Wear your boots for this short hike; they will be useful for crossing Hawk Run. Carry sneakers if you don't want to get your boots wet. The stream bottom is very rocky, and you should not attempt to cross with bare feet.

Bicycles are prohibited on all trails at Hickory Run State Park.

How to Get There
Take exit 274 off I-80 and turn east onto PA 534. Drive through Hickory Run State Park for 9.8 miles; just after you pass under the Pennsylvania Turnpike, park on your right. This is the trailhead for Hawk Falls.

The Trail
Start your hike by crossing the highway and heading east. Walk on the left, facing traffic; the shoulder is wider on this side, and you can see oncoming vehicles. After 600 me-ters turn right, crossing PA 534 to the or-

ganized group camping area. This is the Orchard Trail, although there isn't any sign. Pass a parking lot on your left, which is an alternative trailhead and could be used for a car shuttle if you prefer not to walk on PA 534.

Follow the road through the group camping area. The yellow blazes begin along this road. The trees here are mixed hardwoods—beech, maple, and oak. There is another parking area at the end of the road just before a steel gate. Ignore a yellow-blazed trail from the right and proceed on the road, which is also yellow-blazed.

Beyond the gate, the road becomes grassy, and rhododendrons grow along it. Turn right on trail at a sign for Hawk Falls. The Orchard Trail has been rebuilt by the Pocono Outdoor Club and is easy to follow. There are

occasional glimpses of Mud Run. Note the spruce trees growing along the trail.

At 3.1 km you arrive at the stream for some nice cascades and a small waterfall. This is one of the drops that attract kayakers. The trail crosses ledges of bare rock, then climbs on new switchbacks away from Mud Run. At the top of the slope, turn left along the edge. Avoid the yellow-blazed trail to your right. Black cherry is one of the hardwoods growing here. Turn left at 3.9 km, then right again along the edge, and descend on more switchbacks. Turn right onto the Hawk Falls Trail at 4.1 km. You soon reach a wide side trail to Hawk Falls itself. A scramble over the rocks is required to get a good view of the falls.

After you've seen the falls, return to the trail and the crossing of Hawk Run. The

Rhododendron

stepping-stones are fairly stable, even when they are under water. A stick of some sort is very useful for keeping your balance on them. Stepping-stones must have gaps between them to permit the flow of the stream.

Beyond Hawk Run, continue to PA 534; turn right to return to your car.

Other hiking opportunities abound at Hickory Run. The Boulder Field Trail, (Hike 40), is on the other side of the highway; the Skyline Trail (Hike 33), is back near the park office. Fourth Run Loop (Hike 47) is longer and uses the Fourth Run, Gamewire, and Sand Spring Trails.

The Poconos

32

Camelback Mountain

Location: Near I-80 west of Stroudsburg

Distance: 6.5 km (4.0 miles)

Time: 2½ hourss

Vertical rise: 130 meters (420 feet)

Highlights: Views

Maps: USGS 7½' Mount Pocono; park map

Camelback Mountain is in Big Pocono State Park at the eastern edge of the Poconos. The steep north face of the mountain is used as Camelback Ski Area. The area was purchased by the Pennsylvania Game Commission, but in 1953, 529 hectares became Big Pocono State Park. The remainder, just west of the park, is State Game Lands 38. Since the third edition of this book, the railroad grade has become a de facto ATV trail, and the steep part of the Indian Trail has been closed to prevent erosion. Still, there is some good hiking on top of Camelback. Parts of this hike are rocky, so wear your hiking boots.

How to Get There

The trailhead for this circuit hike is at a parking lot on top of Camelback Mountain. Take exit 299 from I-80 west of Stroudsburg. Turn north on PA 715 for 0.3 mile and then turn left at the light onto Sullivan Road. Avoid reentering I-80 and continue on Sullivan for 1.1 miles. Then turn left onto Camelback Road and drive 4.5 more miles to a parking lot on top of the mountain. Where the Rim Road splits right and left, continue straight ahead to a parking lot at the end of the road near the old stone cottage that once served as the park headquarters.

The Trail

Start your hike by heading back along the road the way you came in, passing the stone cottage and the fire tower. At the time of my visit, climbing the tower was not permitted, but the tower isn't very high and it's hard to see how you could be injured by

32. Camelback Mountain

(P) Parking

View

N

0   1/2 mile

0   1/2 kilometer

To I-80

climbing. Perhaps by the time of your visit this prohibition will have been relaxed. The low-growing trees on the summit consist of pitch pine, scrub oak, and aspen. There is also lots of mountain laurel.

Next, pass the heliport used in suppressing forest fires. The heliport provides a view to the west from Blue Mountain to the edge of the Pocono Plateau. Here you are looking across the entire Ridge and Valley region of the state. At 730 meters you reach a road junction. The south and north parts of the Rim Road come in on your left and right, respectively. Cameltop, at the top of the ski lifts, is just to your right. Continue ahead along the entrance road.

Turn left onto the South Trail at 1.5 km. This trail is also open to bikes and hayburners. Next, bear left on South Trail and pass the white-blazed boundary of State Game Lands 38. Red pine, red oak, and American chestnut are also found along the trail. At 3.3 km a trail to the left leads to the Rim

Road and then to the parking lot where you started; it could be used to truncate your hike. Just beyond this junction is a view south to Wind Gap. Follow this white-birch-lined trail to a junction with the Indian Trail at 4.3 km. Along the way I was delighted to find a very fresh pile of bear scat—so fresh, the flies were still gathering. You will see far more bear sign than actual bears.

Continue straight ahead on a new section of the orange-blazed Indian Trail built by the Keystone Trail Crew in September 2001. Parts of the new trail still contain loose rocks, which you are welcome to remove, but other parts have been seeded and already look as if real Indians could have padded along in their moccasined feet. Note that the Indian Trail is closed to bikes and hayburners. At 5.1 km you reach a junction with the former Indian Trail and the best vista in the Poconos. There are no guardrails at the edge of the cliff, so be careful. At one end you can see the Delaware Water Gap,

The Delaware Water Gap

and as you move along you can see far up into the Poconos toward Tobyhanna State Park and Delaware State Forest. Only a token bit of I-80 is visible.

Continue on the Indian Trail, which is now easier to follow as it passes around and over boulders. Mountain laurel, pitch pine, and scrub oak grow along the trail. Turn right at a large boulder at 5.5 km and continue on a grassy path studded with rocks. This is the first hump of the camel's back. Next, Indian Trail comes in from your left at a convenient bench. (Indian Trail is now a loop.) Then North Trail comes in from your right. At 6.1 km you reach the Rim Road and another view to the right. Continue across the road and parking lot to a trail that leads past a drinking fountain and is then lined with small white birch trees. The trail enters a picnic area and leads to the old concession stand, the former park office, and the parking lot where you left your car. This is the second hump

of the camel's back. Evidently it is a bactrian camel.

At the farthest advance of the last ice sheet, some 15,000 to 20,000 years ago, Camelback formed a promontory into the ice. The ice sheet stretched off to the west and also south to the Delaware Water Gap. It must have been an impressive sight. Camelback is capped with a resistant conglomerate of Devonian age (350 million years ago). Conglomerate looks like concrete in that it is made up of smaller rocks cemented together.

Additional hiking is available here at Big Pocono by following the South Trail east to a junction with the North Trail and then reclimbing Camelback on the North Trail. Another hike in the vicinity of Big Pocono is Mount Minsi in the Delaware Water Gap. A hike in State Game Lands 38, just west of Big Pocono State Park, is described on page 230 of *Pennsylvania Hiking Trails,* 12th edition.

33

Skyline Trail

*Location: Hickory Run State Park,
near the junction of I-80 and I-476*

Distance: 7.8 km (4.9 miles)

Time: 2¾ hours

Vertical rise: 215 meters (700 feet)

Highlights: Mountain stream

*Maps: USGS 7½' Hickory Run;
park map*

Hickory Run State Park, in the western part of the Poconos, is the setting for this hike. This large state park contains a wealth of hiking trails, ranging in length from 400 meters to 10 km, for a total of 60 km. It is not easy to keep up with the maintenance of such a system. In general, the trails here have signs at junctions but are unmarked or poorly blazed. Hikers are relatively invisible park users. They are out on the trails, not at the campground, swimming beach, or picnic area. This contributes to the low priority of trail maintenance.

In general, trails at Hickory Run do not have bridges, and you may have to rock-hop, walk on logs, or just wade across streams. It wouldn't hurt to carry a dry pair of socks in your pack. The stream bottoms are rocky and unkind to bare feet. This hike has one bridgeless crossing of Hickory Run, so you will want your boots.

How to Get There

This hike is in the western part of Hickory Run State Park between PA 534 and the Lehigh River. To reach the park, take exit 274 off I-80 and drive east on PA 534 for 5.2 miles. Park on the right side of PA 534 between the HICKORY RUN TRAIL sign and the bridge over Hickory Run. If you reach the park office, you've gone 0.2 mile too far.

The Trail

To start, follow the highway back to the Hickory Run Trail. There is a well-beaten path outside the guide rail. Use it. Then bear left on the Hickory Run Trail and follow it through a meadow with old apple trees. Yellow birches also grow here. Farther on there are red oaks.

At 1.1 km turn right onto the Skyline Trail and climb the switchbacks up the side of the valley. This is a real trail, not an old road, and it is marked with occasional blue diamonds nailed to the trees. There are six switchbacks to the top of the hill.

At the crest the trail goes straight ahead, away from the edge. Ignore two double blazes to the right of the trail at this point; they mark the site of a blowdown that has since rotted away. The footway is easy to

follow. Soon there is a blue paint blaze. The blazing is inadequate to follow this trail, but it's nice to have occasional confirmation that you are still on it.

Next, you pass through an upland meadow with a sparse growth of birch trees. Then cross Goulds Run and Trail and reach a junction of two versions of the Skyline Trail at 2.3 km. You could extend your hike by taking the right-hand version, which intersects the Fire Lane Trail farther to the north than this hike does.

Continue ahead at this junction through the upland meadow. Note the ground pine and ground cedar along the way. Then cross

Hickory Run

a woods road followed by an intermittent stream.

At 3.4 km turn left onto the Fire Lane Trail. (The extended version of this hike reenters here.) Then cross the same stream. There is a considerable amount of up and down along the Fire Lane. Pass an old apple tree and reach the top of the first hill. Ignore a woods road that enters from your left. There is a meadow to your right with occasional views of the Lehigh River below. Note the bluebird houses in the meadow.

Cross Goulds Run and Trail. Anglers use Goulds Run Trail to reach the Lehigh. Then climb again. At 5.4 km cross Hickory Run as best you can, then turn left onto the Hickory Run Trail—a beautiful old road grade through hemlocks and rhododendrons.

Next, you reach a junction with the Sand Spring Trail. An Eagle Scout project has produced a footbridge across Hickory Run at this point. This hike turns left and crosses Hickory Run on this new bridge. Shortly, you reach the junction with the Skyline Trail. Retrace your steps on the Hickory Run Trail to PA 534 and your car.

There are additional hikes in Hickory Run State Park on the Boulder Field Trail (Hike 40), as well as around Hawk Falls (Hike 31), and Fourth Run (Hike 47). The new footbridge over Hickory Run permits a short circuit hike using the Hickory Run Trail on one side of the run and Sand Spring Trail on the other.

34

Blooming Grove Trail

Location: North of exit 8 off I-84

Distance: 7.9 km (4.9 miles)

Time: 3 hours

Vertical rise: 90 meters (300 feet)

Highlights: Stream, wildflowers

Maps: USGS 7½' Hawley; forestry map

The Blooming Grove Trail is located in Delaware State Forest on PA 402 between I-84 and US 6. It consists of a Red Loop and a longer Blue Loop connected by the White Deer Trail. It was built by the 4-H Club of Pike County in 1975, in cooperation with the Bureau of Forestry. Since being reopened by Keystone Trails Association volunteers in April 1993, the trails are now maintained by volunteers from the Pocono Outdoor Club.

This hike is on an often rocky and sometimes wet trail, so wear your hiking boots. The pathway is almost flat but leads through surprisingly varied terrain.

How to Get There

Take exit 30 off I-84 and head north on PA 402 for 3.9 miles. There is a large parking lot, marked with a sign, on the west side of the highway. This parking area is about 1 mile south of US 6.

The Trail

The Blooming Grove Trail System is bisected by a double power line. To start the hike, head down the gated dirt road from the parking lot along this line and turn right to a mapboard at the edge of the woods. The red blazes start here. Bear right at a junction of red-marked trails at 230 meters. Soon you can see Blue Heron Swamp to the left. Next, cross a stream on logs. Look for fiddlehead ferns here in spring.

Turn right onto the white-blazed White Deer Trail at 1 km. This junction is marked

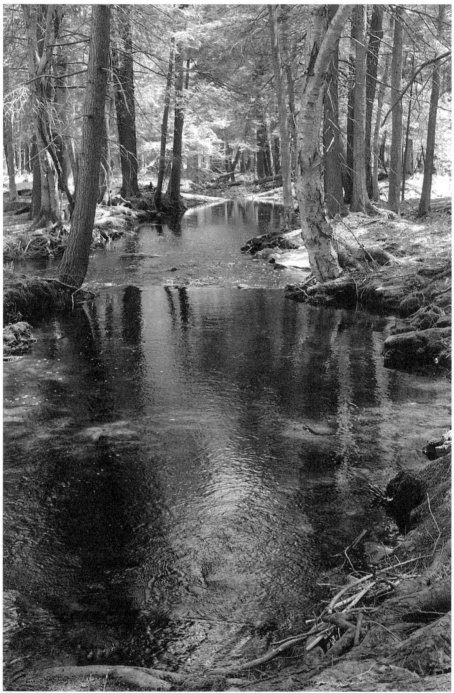

Gates Meadow Run

with a trail register. So far the route has been through mixed hardwoods—mostly black birches and oaks. Spring wildflowers along the trail are violets, fringed polygalas, and coneflowers.

At 1.3 km turn left onto the blue-blazed Gates Meadow Loop. Cross a stream on rocks and pass some vernal ponds. Look for tiny hop toads along this section. The trail then enters white pines. Bracken grows here, along with highbush blueberries and mayapples.

Cross another stream. Shadbush are found here, and many small ones can be seen on the forest floor. Shadbush flowers in early spring, when the shad used to swim up the rivers to spawn—hence the name. Dams and pollution have now all but eliminated this annual migration.

Walk under the power line at 3.2 km. Cross a wet area on stepping-stones, then bear right along Gates Meadow Run. This area is particularly attractive, with an open stand of hemlocks along the stream. Enter a meadow with some spruce and turn left onto a grassy road. Cross the run on a culvert. The water looks as if someone has made tea with it; this is due to iron tannate from the swamps and bogs that are drained by the run.

Turn left into the hemlocks and move upstream along the same run; turn right at 4.2 km. In low water you might be able to cross the run at this point, thus avoiding a downstream detour to the culvert.

Next, turn left onto the grassy road. In mid-May the road is an azure carpet of bluets. Pass a clearing and turn left onto another grassy road next to PA 402.

Keep left through a wet area at 5 km, followed by the big climb of the day—about 40 meters long. Turn right on trail at 5.2 km. There is a view of Gates Meadow Run to your left. Note the sheep laurel growing along the trail; it is smaller than mountain laurel but blooms at about the same time in June. Cross another wet area and jog left on a jeep road. There are a lot of black spruces growing along this section. Then enter hardwoods again.

Turn left onto the white-blazed White Deer Trail at 6.3 km. In spring look for painted trilliums. Cross the power-line swath and look for wild strawberries. After entering the woods you could find an obscure junction with a shortcut on a red-blazed trail to your right; this hike continues on the white blazes, however. Cross the outlet from Blue Heron Swamp on stones, and climb briefly.

Turn right onto the red-blazed trail at the trail register and retrace your steps to your car.

Additional hiking opportunities can be found on the Thunder Swamp Trail (Hike 45) and at Promised Land State Park (Hike 44) and the Bruce Lake Natural Area (Hike 42). For a free trail map of the Blooming Grove Trail, write to Delaware State Forest, HC 1, Box 95A, Swiftwater, PA 18370-9723; or call 570-895-4000.

35

Mount Minsi

Location: In Delaware Water Gap

Distance: 7.9 km (4.9 miles)

Time: 3 hours

Vertical rise: 310 meters (1,020 feet)

Highlights: Views

Map: USGS 7½' Stroudsburg; KTA sections 1–6

Mount Minsi is on the Pennsylvania side of the Delaware Water Gap. It is not as imposing as Mount Tammany in New Jersey, but it makes a better hike. This section of Kittatinny Mountain is part of the Delaware Water Gap National Recreation Area. The recreation area was to be centered on the Tocks Island Dam, but that would have flooded the valley up to New York State. Other plans were for a scenic highway that would have destroyed the Appalachian Trail (AT) between Tott's Gap and the Delaware River. Protests, some led by Supreme Court justice William O. Douglas, halted these plans. The national recreation area now protects the free-flowing Delaware River for us to enjoy.

Mount Minsi is part of the Shawangunk formation, containing coarse-grained sandstones and conglomerates of Silurian age (about 400 million years old). Farther west parts of this formation are known as the Tuscarora sandstone; they extend to North Fork Mountain in West Virginia. To the north, the formation extends to the Shawangunk Mountains in New York State.

This is a circuit hike using the AT and the Mount Minsi fire road. Wear your hiking boots, as the AT is notoriously rough and rocky. Pennsylvania has the rockiest footway of all the 14 states on the AT; these rocks have turned many an ankle, including one of mine.

Northbound through-hikers should reach the Delaware River in mid- to late June. Given the steep slopes here, you may have an opportunity to try the M&M test for through-hik-

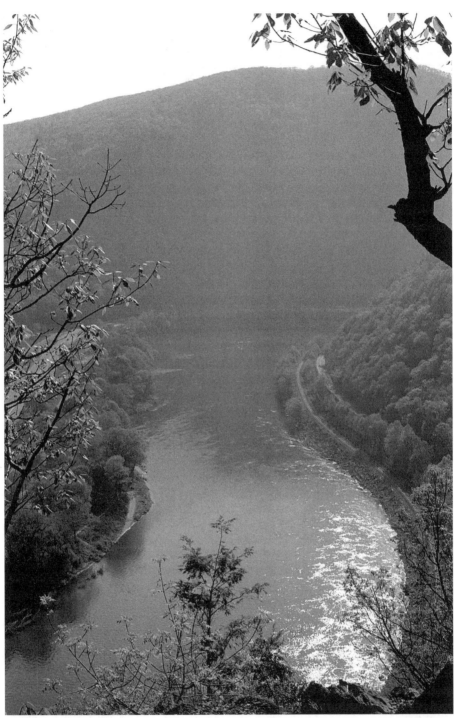

The Delaware Water Gap

ers: Drop an M&M on the ground. A day-hiker will pick it up and put it in his trash bag. A backpacker will wipe it off and eat it. A through-hiker will chase it down the mountainside.

How to Get There

From exit 310 off I-80, drive 0.6 mile to the traffic light in the town of Delaware Water Gap. Turn left (south) onto PA 611 and go 0.3 mile. Then turn right at the Deer Head Inn onto Mountain Road; drive 0.2 mile to the Lake Lenape parking lot. Note the white blazes along Mountain Road, which show that it is part of the AT.

The Trail

From the parking lot, follow the white blazes past the gate on the Mount Minsi fire road. Just around the corner you cross the dam forming Lake Lenape, a picturesque small impoundment. Then the fire road passes cliffs to the right, and at 600 meters you follow the AT as it turns left on trail under hemlocks. Soon there is a view to your left of the Delaware, including the I-80 bridge. This bridge may be the scariest part of the AT; it shakes up and down whenever an 18-wheeler goes by.

Next, you encounter rhododendrons and hemlocks. Note that most of the hemlocks here look sick, presumably from the woolly adelgid, an aphid that sucks the juices from the hemlock needles, weakening the trees. Some trees die immediately; the larger specimens will provide picturesque snags for years to come. Others soldier on, but no one knows whether they will survive. The biodiversity of Penn's Woods is taking another hit.

Cross a larger stream on rocks at 1.8 km. This is the outlet for Lake Latini. At 2 km there is another view of the Water Gap, but note that the AT switchbacks to the right just before this view. Follow the blazes carefully, as the trail crosses open areas; sometimes the blazes are painted on the rock underfoot.

There is another view of the Gap before the AT enters a tunnel through the rhododendrons.

Note the well-made water bars on this section. Some are made of rocks and others, logs. The purpose of a water bar is to deflect water off the trail. This means the upper edge must be cleared whenever it fills up with sand and mud. A well-made water bar is a thing of beauty and a chore forever.

The climb eases off before you jog left across the Mount Minsi fire road at 3 km. You reach your last view of the Gap at 3.3 km. Pitch pines and shadbush grow around these rocks, along with the only healthy hemlock I saw on this hike. From here you can see the cliffs and the other side of Mount Tammany; you can also see up Dunnfield Creek on the New Jersey side of the river. This is the last view, but not the summit. If you are a peak-bagger, continue along the AT for another 400 meters to the foundations of a fire tower. (The excursion to this, the actual summit, is included in this hike's mileage.)

While I was looking at the spruce trees growing at the summit, I noticed a movement at the edge of the brush. It was a bear—the only bear I've ever seen on the AT. When I made a motion for my camera, it vanished into the woods.

Turn back along the AT, but when you reach the Mount Minsi fire road, bear right. Cross the AT again and continue down over ledges of bedrock. At various junctions along the way, just continue straight ahead. At 5 km pass a spring to your left. Black birch grows along the fire road. At 6.8 km there is a road to your left. It leads to a view of the Gap from a bluff, but is not included in this hike. The junction is marked only by some rusty culvert pipes. Next, the AT comes in from your right, and, finally, you pass Lake Lenape to reach the parking lot.

There is additional hiking at Big Pocono State Park, just a few exits up I-80 (see Hike 32).

36

Dingmans Falls

Location: 10 miles south of Milford

Distance: 8.0 km (4.9 miles)

Time: 4 hours

Vertical rise: 160 meters (525 feet)

Highlights: Waterfalls

Map: USGS 7½' Lake Maskenozha

An obscure item in a tourist brochure sent me on a search for this hike. The brochure claimed there was a "five mile" hike at Dingmans Falls. But standard hiking references list only 0.5 mile there, and less than 2 miles at the George W. Childs Recreation Area farther upstream. I finally found the hike; it consists of the section of Dingmans Creek between the two areas.

The trail is unmarked, unmaintained, and un-built—yet it is easy to follow. All you have to do is keep the creek in sight. The woods are fairly open and in many places a footway has been worn into the ground, but this is a trail for the more adventurous hiker. Note that only the south bank of Dingmans Creek is public property. Private enclaves remain on the north bank, the property of hostile landowners.

The ideal time for this hike is a few days after a heavy rain. Beware of subfreezing weather, when spray from the falls can cover the steps and walkways with ice. There is some steep hillside walking on this hike, so wear your boots.

If it's open, take a look at the exhibits in the visitors center. These exhibits deal with the area's wildlife and geology. How did the Delaware Water Gap National Recreation Area get so many waterfalls? During the ice age, a river of ice deepened and widened the Delaware River Valley. It also confused the preglacial drainage system. When the ice melted, the new streams flowing off the Pocono Plateau flowed over cliffs to get to the Delaware Valley. Waterfalls are generally transient on a geologic time scale; these date from the most recent ice age, only 15,000 to

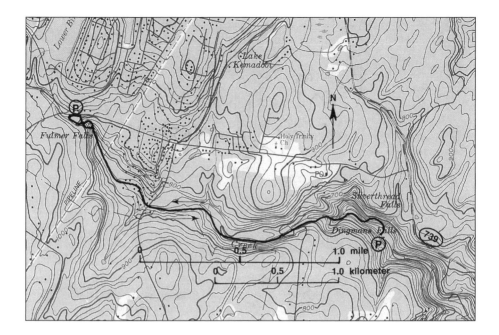

20,000 years ago. Waterfalls erode back upstream, creating a narrow canyon below.

How to Get There

This hike is written as an in-and-out hike, but it could also be done as a car shuttle. If you elect the latter option, first leave one car at the George W. Childs Recreation Area. To get there, from the traffic light at the junction of US 209 and PA 739, drive north on PA 739 for 1.1 miles. Then turn left onto Silver Lake Road, which is the first paved road on your left. After another 1.7 miles you reach the recreation site. There are two parking areas. Leave one car here and return to the junction of US 209 and PA 739. Turn south onto US 209. At 0.1 mile from the light, turn right onto Johnny Bee Road. After 0.4 mile turn right onto Dingmans Falls Road; it is another 0.8 mile to the visitors center and parking lot.

The Trail

Start your hike from the visitors center and cross the bridge over Dingmans Creek. Immediately you are at the foot of Silver Thread Falls, a narrow waterfall that has eroded along joint fractures in shale. Shale erodes relatively easily.

Then move on and cross the creek again. Turn right through a tunnel in the rhododendron (it blooms the first 2 weeks in July). Soon you reach the platform at the base of Dingmans Falls. The 40-meter fall cascades down shale ledges.

Now turn back and take the steps to the upper platform, crossing another bridge over a side stream. The upper platform is at the brink of Dingmans Falls. This is as far as most people go, but it is where the adventurous part of this hike begins.

Look for a path up the ledges, worn over the hemlock roots, and follow it. Soon your way becomes easier, but keep well above the creek. (You wouldn't want to slip and fall in, because swimming is prohibited this close to the falls.)

Since this trail is not blazed or maintained, there are frequently two or even three footways at different levels. Some of them are so wide that they look like somebody has actually done the required sidehill construction with Pulaskis and mattocks.

Soon the slope eases off and you can descend closer to the stream. At 1.2 km you cross Doodle Hollow Road. It is blocked to traffic at the bridge. Do not cross this bridge; there is private land on the other side.

Later you reach an old grade that descends to the stream. Note that there is a ford here where people used to drive across.

The woods are open and the few blowdowns can be detoured or stepped over, but most of the trees are hemlocks. The woolly adelgid, an insect pest accidentally introduced, has already invaded the Delaware recreation area. It feeds on hemlocks and eventually kills them. If it were to kill the hemlocks here, brush would grow up and the valley would soon be blocked with blowdowns. On my most recent visit the hemlocks appeared to have been savaged by the woolly adelgid but were still alive. Why aren't they dead?

At 2.6 km cross SR 2001, a paved road that to your right heads to Silver Lake Road and PA 739. Do not cross this bridge. Follow an old road briefly, but when it veers away from the creek, bear right and return to the bank. At 3.3 km cross a pipeline swath. Another 100 meters brings you to the first bridge in the Childs park. This last bit is the steepest and hardest part of the hike.

Cross this bridge to get a good view of Deer Leap Falls. Then climb to its brink and cross again. Continue upstream and cross yet another bridge, below Fulmer Falls. Continue to Factory Falls. The crumbling stone walls are the postindustrial ruins of a factory that once got waterpower from Dingmans Creek. Cross a bridge above Factory Falls. There are no more falls above this point, so turn downstream, crossing bridges in the opposite direction.

There are one too many bridges for this plan to work out. Be sure that you end up on the *south* side of Dingmans Creek at the last bridge below Deer Leap Falls. (This is the right side as you face downstream.) Proceed downstream and retrace your steps to the visitors center and your car.

We are used to the roar of traffic, the roar of airplanes, the roar of machinery. A waterfall is a natural roar. As John Muir said, "As long as I live I'll hear waterfalls and birds sing and get as near the heart of the world as I can."

37

Lakeside Trail

Location: Near I-380 south of Scranton

Distance: 8.3 km (5.2 miles)

Time: 2½ hours

Vertical rise: 25 meters (80 feet)

Highlights: Lake

Maps: USGS 7½' Tobyhanna; park map

Tobyhanna State Park on PA 423 outside the town of Tobyhanna is the site of this hike. The Lakeside Trail is a hardened path for hiking and bicycling in summer, snowmobiling and cross-country skiing in winter. It circles Tobyhanna Lake, formed by the damming of Tobyhanna Creek. This is a very easy trail to hike, and you can look around to see things; you don't have to keep looking at the ground, as you do on most trails.

Tobyhanna State Park is part of the former Tobyhanna Military Reservation, which was used as an artillery range up through World War II. The area still contains unexploded shells; some are found every year. The trails have been cleared, so this concern arises only for off-trail hikers. If you should find a shell, don't pick it up; mark its position as best you can and report it to the park office. Let the bomb disposal squad take care of the shell.

The Lakeside Trail is wheelchair-accessible, and some adventurous handicapped people have completed the entire trail. Walking shoes are fine for this hike's excellent footway, but you still may have to skirt a puddle or two.

How to Get There

Tobyhanna State Park is most easily reached from exit 8 off I-380. Take PA 423 north for about 3 miles to the park. You can also reach the park from exit 20 off I-84; follow PA 507, PA 191, and PA 423 for a total of 12 miles. At the entrance to the park, turn left for the day-use area. Park in area 2 or 3.

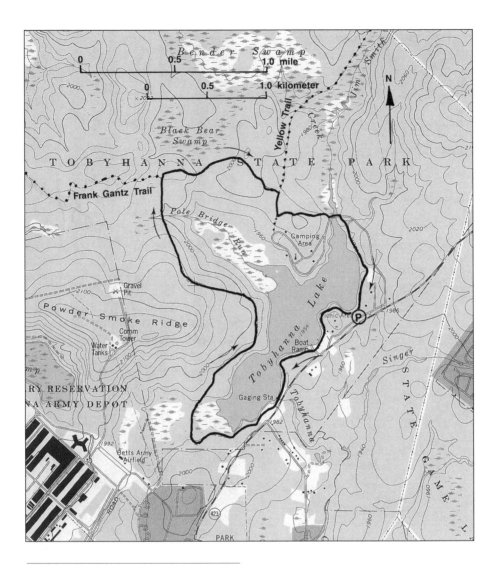

The Trail

Make your way to the bathhouse. Bear left past the water pump and continue on the surfaced trail, which follows the shore of Tobyhanna Lake around a point to the boat-launching and -mooring area. The trail is blue-blazed except right near the bathhouse. Keep right to stay on it. Watch for evidence of beaver activity in the form of sticks with the bark chewed off or trees that

have been felled. Here the Lakeside Trail is lined with rhododendrons.

At 1.4 km you reach the dam; keep left and use the footbridge to cross the outlet. (Hikers are not permitted to use the walkway over the dam.) Then bear right and pass a vehicle gate to continue. Note the spruce growing along the trail. Beech is abundant, and there are black cherry, yellow birch, white birch, and red maple trees.

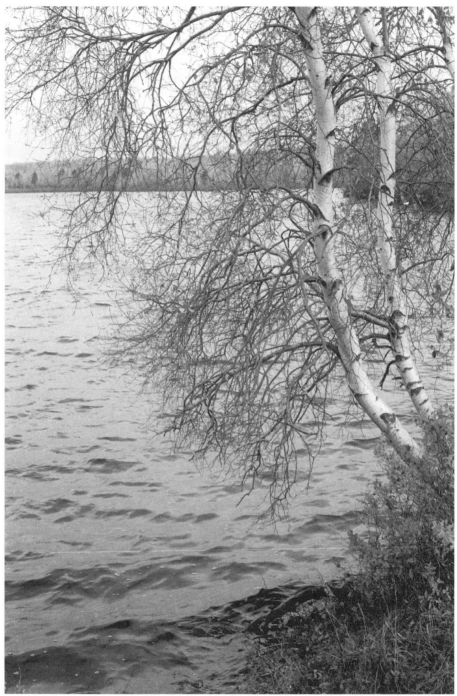

Tobyhanna Lake

Picnic tables are found along the way if you care to rest or eat lunch.

At 3.7 km you turn left, away from the lake. The trail is also equipped with mileposts set for snowmobiles, which circle the lake in the opposite direction. The muted roar of I-380, about 3 km away, can be heard.

Cross Pole Bridge Run on a substantial bridge at 5 km, and reach the junction with the red-blazed Frank Gantz Trail at 5.4 km. The Frank Gantz Trail connects with trails in Gouldsboro State Park, 5 km away. Blazed but not maintained, it could be used for a car-shuttle hike—or to combine this hike with the one at Gouldsboro (Hike 38) and create a 26 km boot-buster.

Turn right on the blue blazes. At 6.5 km you reach a junction with the Yellow Trail.

(This goes left 5.3 km all the way to PA 196, but it crosses Tobyhanna Creek without benefit of a bridge. The creek may be all but impassable in high water, but would make an inviting side trip in low water.)

Turn right on the blue blazes, then left to reach a parking lot at milepost 0, the start of the one-way snowmobile trail. Turn left onto the paved road and cross a bridge consisting of five culverts over Tobyhanna Creek.

At 7.4 km turn right onto the Lakeside Trail and follow it back to the bathhouse and your car. In-season, take time for a swim.

Besides the Frank Gantz and Yellow Trails at Tobyhanna, there is additional hiking in nearby Gouldsboro State Park (see Hike 38).

38

Gouldsboro State Park

Location: Near I-380 south of Scranton

Distance: 9.1 km (5.6 miles)

Time: 3 hours

Vertical rise: 91 meters (300 feet)

Highlights: Pocono swamp

Maps: USGS 7½' Tobyhanna; park map

In 1949 Pennsylvania received title to 10,500 hectares from the federal government. This land had been part of the Tobyhanna Military Reservation. A third of the land was split between Tobyhanna and Gouldsboro State Parks, while the balance became State Game Lands 127.

Gouldsboro Park is named for the nearby town of Gouldsboro, which in turn was named for railroad magnate Jay Gould. At one time Gould owned 10 percent of all the railroads in the country, including the Erie-Lackawanna, which separates the two parks. This railroad is now part of Steamtown USA and is used for excursions from Scranton to Pocono Summit. Gould was also co-owner of a nearby tannery.

Although parts of this hike are on old roads, the Prospect Rock Trail is rough and rocky, requiring your boots. In addition, there is a challenging crossing of the outlet from Kistler Swamp.

How to Get There

Take exit 13 off I-380 and drive north on PA 507 for 2.1 miles. Turn south onto the park road and go 1 mile; turn left into parking lot 1. Gouldsboro can also be reached from exit 20 off I-84 by driving about 8 miles south on PA 507.

The Trail

Pick up the blue-blazed Prospect Rock Trail and head north on an old road, easy walking. At 500 meters turn left on trail to reach State Park Road. Cross the road, step over the guide rail, and turn right. Follow the road

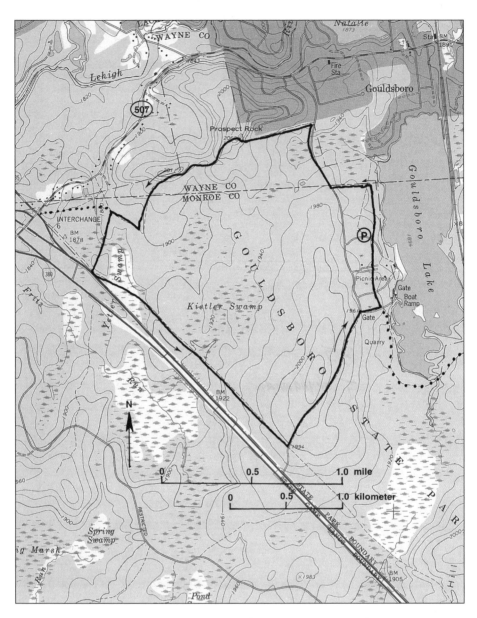

to 1.5 km, where you turn left onto a very rocky trail that follows the northern boundary of the park. At several places you can look into backyards of houses built across the boundary on private land.

After the park boundary turns north, climb steeply over rocks to Prospect Rock

(elevation: 628 meters). There may have been a view to the south from here at one time, but the trees have grown up. Beyond, the trail descends gently, but the footway remains rocky.

At 3.6 km turn sharply right onto an old road. At last you have a good footway. Then

Old 611

turn left at the junction with the red-blazed Connector Trail. At 4.2 km you reach the outlet from Kistler Swamp. Cross here as best you can. On the far side of the stream, the footway becomes a watercourse in wet times, but at 4.5 km you reach Old 611 and turn left. The Connector Trail comes in from your right.

Old 611 is the remains of a paved two-lane highway that was replaced by I-380. The concrete is cracked, buckled, and broken now. As it heads south across Kistler Swamp, it has been reduced to a single lane by encroaching brush. Swamps such as this are a feature of the Poconos, a mighty fortress for black bears when they are hunted. No hunter would penetrate such a swamp very far, so the Poconos have the most secure bear population in the state. Beyond the swamp Old 611 gently climbs a hill with aspen trees.

As you hike down Old 611, ask yourself how much of our country is polluted with traffic noise. Pennsylvania is said to have more miles of highway than any other state except Texas—which is five times as large. Perhaps we could abandon some more. They make such nice trails after a couple of decades.

At 6.8 km turn left onto the old park entrance road, which was severed to the west by I-380. There is a picnic table at this junction. The old entrance road is in better shape than Old 611, although they must have been abandoned at the same time.

Continue to 8.2 km, where you pass a gate and turn right onto a paved road to the boat launch. Next, turn left where the red-blazed Frank Gantz Trail comes in from Tobyhanna State Park. Walk through the picnic area, crossing several parking areas, to area 1, where you left your car.

Additional hiking is available at nearby Tobyhanna State Park (see Hike 37). The Frank Gantz Trail between the two parks is also available.

39

Choke Creek Trail

Location: 12 miles east of Wilkes-Barre

Distance: 10.0 km (6.2 miles)

Time: 3¼ hours

Vertical rise: 90 meters (290 feet)

Highlights: Mountain stream

Maps: USGS 7½' Pleasant View Summit, Thornhurst; Pinchot Trail map

Choke Creek Nature Trail is on the southern part of the Pinchot Trail in Lackawanna State Forest. The Pinchot Trail System was laid out by Frank Gantz, a retired truck driver, back in the 1970s. He explored the area, finding old trails and new routes, determining where the trail should go.

As usual, there are lots of wet spots and more than a few rocks on the trail, so your hiking boots are in order.

How to Get There

For directions to the Pinchot Trail, see Hike 46.

If you are coming from I-380 or I-80, turn left onto Tannery Road just 0.1 mile north of the junction of Pine Grove and Bear Lake Roads. From I-81, continue 2.4 miles past the Pinchot trailhead and turn right onto Tannery Road. In either case, drive 1.9 miles to a parking area on the left with a large sign proclaiming CHOKE CREEK NATURE TRAIL. On Tannery Road you will cross the blue blazes of the main Pinchot Trail. The length of Choke Creek Trail is greater than is advertised on the sign.

The Trail

Start down the orange-blazed trail that leads directly away from the road; it follows the boundary of state forest land. Along the way you pass mountain and sheep laurel (both bloom in June), rhododendron (blooms in July), black spruce, and white pine.

Turn left at 600 meters and detour around a bog. Here there are many highbush blueberries. They ripen in July, but

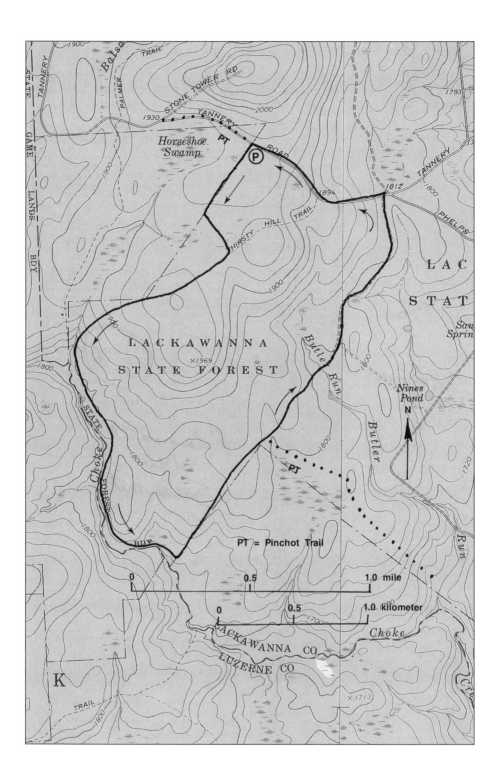

PT = Pinchot Trail

| 0 | 0.5 | 1.0 mile |
| 0 | 0.5 | 1.0 kilometer |

many of the berry pickers wear fur coats, even in summer.

Turn right at 1.2 km and pass pitch pine, black gum, red maple, black birch, and sassafras. The leaves of sassafras are quite variable. Some leaves are elliptical, while others are mitten-shaped—both left-handed and right-handed. Some leaves even have "thumbs" on both sides.

Cross a stream on stepping-stones at 1.8 km, and turn left at a campsite. In May look for painted trillium along the trail. Also listen for the towhee, or woods robin. Towhees scratch noisily among the dead leaves on the forest floor. Their most frequent call is a loud *chewink,* but at times they will sing *drink your tea,* with the "tea" trilled.

Now beech trees, another northern hardwood, make their appearance along the trail. Beech leaves are sometimes confused with American chestnut leaves but tend to be shorter.

At 3.5 km turn downstream along a tributary of Choke Creek. Immediately you reach the main stream at a beaver pond; you can see the beaver house. Part of a footbridge has been incorporated into the dam. At one point the pond has flooded the trail, and you must detour around it. A blazed tree is now surrounded by water, too. Choke Creek is alleged to harbor native brook trout.

Turn right at 3.9 km, passing one campsite, then another, farther along. Neither satisfies the requirement that campsites be at least 50 meters from any trail. Pass a large hemlock at 5 km and then what looks like an old burn area.

After passing another campsite at the edge of a pool, turn left and climb away from the creek along a posted boundary of private land. Cross a stream on stepping-stones and reach a junction with the Butler Run Trail at 6.8 km. The orange-blazed main trail of the Pinchot system turns right here, but you continue ahead on a red-blazed trail. Cross Butler Run at 7.5 km, and turn left onto a grassy road at 7.8 km.

Suddenly a small, furry black animal darts across the trail ahead. It's a bear cub trying to catch up with its family. Leave bear cubs alone. The mother is not far off. No matter how cute it is, don't touch the cub. If it smells "wrong," its mother may abandon it. Bear adoptions are difficult to arrange, and a cub raised in captivity is sentenced to a life behind bars.

Along the grassy swath, you pass parts of the Howley Orienteering Area. This area was developed by a local search-and-rescue expert to teach skills required to avoid getting lost in the woods. At 9 km pass a steel gate and turn left onto Tannery Road. It is another 1 km back to your car.

The Pinchot Trail System provides lots of other hiking opportunities, particularly circuit hikes. See the Painter Creek Loop (Hike 46), for example.

40

Boulder Field

Location: Hickory Run State Park, near the junction of I-80 and I-476

Distance: 11.3 km (7.0 miles)

Time: 4 hours

Vertical rise: 170 meters (560 feet)

Highlights: Boulder field

*Maps: USGS 7½' Hickory Run;
park map*

The existence of Hickory Run State Park is due to Colonel H. C. Trexler, who purchased more than 5,000 hectares at tax sales after logging for timber and hemlock bark was completed in 1912. The National Park Service was able to acquire much of the park from his estate. During the 1930s this park and four others were operated as demonstration recreation areas by the National Park Service. In 1945 Hickory Run was deeded to the state of Pennsylvania. Other large parks in the state—Blue Knob, French Creek, Laurel Hill, Raccoon Creek— were acquired in the same manner. At 6,250 hectares, Hickory Run is the largest state park in the Poconos and, indeed, in eastern Pennsylvania.

It encompasses the boulder field that is your destination for this hike. The field was produced 15,000 to 20,000 years ago, when the glacial front of the last ice age was about 1.5 km to the northeast. (The terminal moraine of the Wisconsin ice sheet passes through Hickory Run.) The climate must have been like that of parts of Greenland near its ice cap today. Freezing and thawing would have been severe during summer; water seeping into cracks would have frozen every night, wedging the rocks apart. Subsequent water erosion has removed any sand and gravel, leaving only the boulders.

How to Get There

To reach the trailhead, take exit 274 off I-80 and turn east onto PA 534. Turn left in Lehigh Tannery and continue across a section of State Game Lands 40. Then enter

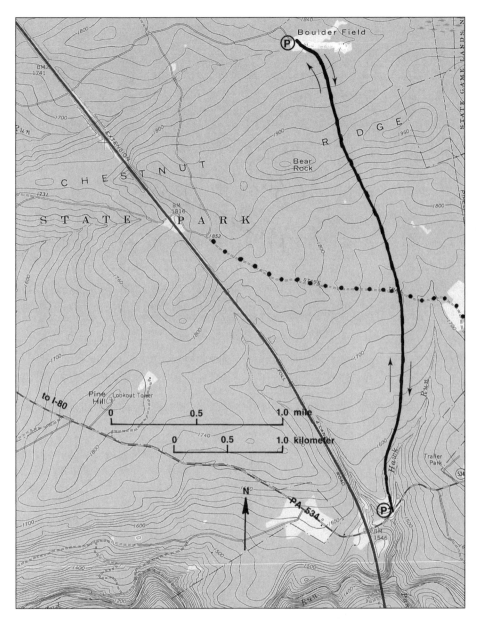

Hickory Run State Park, passing the park office. Immediately after passing under the Pennsylvania Turnpike, park on the left side of the highway at 9.8 miles.

Hickory Run State Park can also be reached from exit 95 off the Pennsylvania Turnpike, I-476, by driving west 3 miles on PA 940 and then east on PA 534.

The distance, time, and vertical rise in the heading assume that you take this hike on an in-and-out basis, but if you have two cars available, you can also do it as a car-shuttle

The boulder field

hike by leaving a car at the Boulder Field parking area. To reach this area, follow a park road that leaves PA 534 from a spot 0.5 mile east of the park office. The drive is 7.9 miles.

The Trail

The Boulder Field Trail leaves from the corner of the parking area on PA 534. The trail heads up a flight of steps and then crosses an old apple orchard before entering the woods. It's unblazed but wide and easy to follow as it slowly diverges from the roar of the turnpike. Trees along the way are beech, black cherry, red maple, hemlock, yellow birch, black gum, and a very occasional red oak—typical mixed hardwoods. There are scattered clumps of rhododendrons along the first part of the trail. It is a very pleasant walk through the woods, although the footway is rocky. Farther along there are scattered hemlocks.

You cross the Stage Trail at 2.5 km. Once a stage route from Philadelphia to Wilkes-Barre, today it is a wide trail that traverses the park. However, it is open to vehicles.

Beyond the Stage Trail, the Boulder Field Trail becomes narrower, crosses a watercourse, and passes through patches of mountain laurel. Hemlocks become more numerous. Spruce, black gum, and white pine trees are also passed. Under the white pines, stop and listen to the wind in the treetops.

The official trail description says there is a steady uphill slope, but it is scarcely noticeable. At 4.4 km you cross the flat top of Chestnut Ridge and start to descend very gently through a dense stand of hemlocks into the headwaters of Hickory Run itself. You can also see old yellow and red paint blazes along the trail.

The edge of the boulder field is reached at 5.3 km. The field occupies a relatively flat valley at the headwaters of Hickory Run. Sometimes water can be heard running underneath the rocks.

As you head out into the field, take a good look at where you emerged from the woods. On my last hike this spot was marked only by a signboard leaning against a tree. You will need to find this trailhead to return to your car. The listed distance takes you clear across the field to the parking lot, where your other car will be if you did this hike as a shuttle. Otherwise, retrace your steps down the Boulder Field Trail to your car on PA 534.

Other hiking opportunities abound at Hickory Run State Park, as there are 60 km of trails. In particular, see Hawk Falls (Hike 31), Skyline Trail (Hike 33), and Fourth Run Loop (Hike 47).

41

Pennel Run

Location: West of PA 402, north of Stroudsburg

Distance: 11.4 km (7.1 miles)

Time: 4¼ hours

Vertical rise: 220 meters (730 feet)

Highlights: Natural area

Maps: USGS 7½' Twelvemile Pond, Skytop; Thunder Swamp Trail System map

The Thunder Swamp Trail System (TSTS) in the Delaware State Forest provides more than 70 km of hiking trails. The system includes an orange-blazed loop trail and numerous red-blazed side trails, and provides recreational opportunities in rapidly growing Pike County.

The Pennel Run Natural Area consists of 380 hectares of aspens, black birches, and mixed oaks. Much of Utts Swamp lies within the natural area.

This hike also visits Spruce Run, which flows east of the natural area. Like most other streams in the Poconos, its tea-colored waters flow through a corridor of hemlocks.

This portion of the Thunder Swamp Trail is unusually rocky, so wear your hiking boots.

How to Get There

You can reach the trailhead from exit 30 off I-84 by driving south on PA 402 for 14.7 miles, passing Porters Lake and the Burnt Mills trailhead of the TSTS. Turn right onto Snow Hill Road and follow it for 2.4 miles to a parking lot on the right.

You can also reach Snow Hill Road from exit 309 off I-80. Follow US 209 north to Marshalls Creek and turn onto PA 402. Follow PA 402 north, passing the main TSTS trailhead, and turn left onto Snow Hill Road after about 10.5 miles.

The Trail

Turn right onto paved Snow Hill Road and go 50 meters, then turn right again onto the orange-blazed main trail. Pass a trail register and an American chestnut sprout. After

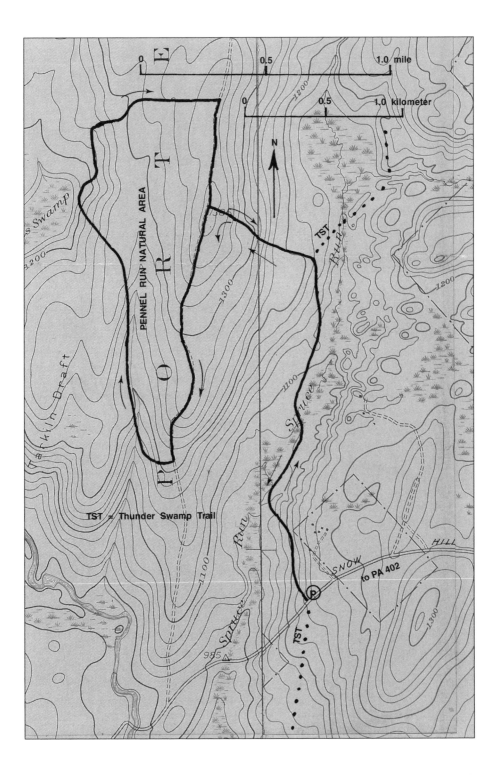

0 E T 0.5 1.0 mile

0 0.5 1.0 kilometer

N

PENNEL RUN NATURAL AREA

P O R T E

1200

1300

1100

Swamp

1200

Larkin Draft

1100

1100

985

Spruce Run

Snyce Run

R.R.

TST

SNOW HILL

to PA 402

1200

1300

TST

P

TST = Thunder Swamp Trail

The bridge over Spruce Run

the logging of the 19th century, the Appalachians returned to hardwoods. From Maine to Georgia, every other tree was an American chestnut. Then came the chestnut blight, an imported fungus. The blight does not kill the below-ground portions of the tree, so stumps continue to send up new shoots even today. Indeed, the abundance of these shoots keeps the chestnut from being designated an endangered species! However, many experts suspect that the old chestnut stumps are now about to die. Then the American chestnut—an ideal forest tree with wood for both rough and fine construction and nuts for both people and wildlife—will be extinct at last. Perhaps then it can be classed as endangered.

At 800 meters pass some large white pines. Beech, shagbark hickory, tulip, and hemlock also grow here. Spruce Run can be seen to your left. There is some poison ivy along the trail near Spruce Run.

Cross a side stream and come to a bridge over Spruce Run. This bridge was built by volunteers in the Trail Care Project of the Keystone Trails Association (KTA). The first year they carried in wire baskets, called gabions, and filled them with locally grown rocks. The gabions stood here for 11 months before Trail Care was able to return and finish the bridge.

Continue on the orange blazes and climb gently to an intersection at 2.6 km, marked by a trail sign. All the trail signs along this hike were made by KTA volunteers; many were installed by an expedition in April 1991.

Turn left on red blazes at this junction and climb gently, except for a ledge, to Hay Road. This trail is so straight that it must have been a fire lane in the early days of the state forests. Hay Road is red-blazed in both directions and forms the eastern boundary of the Pennel Run Natural Area. Turn left and follow this delightful old road along the crest of the ridge. In May look for wild azaleas and pink lady's slippers.

Turn right onto a trail at 4.8 km and follow it down to Pennel Run, which you cross on moss-covered rocks. On the far side, turn upstream and follow blazes carefully. The trail crosses another ridge and descends to the edge of Utts Swamp. It then climbs back up the ridge to Hay Road at 7.7 km. Turn right and close the loop at 8 km. Turn left onto the old fire lane and retrace your steps to your car, remembering to turn right on the orange blazes.

Other hiking opportunities nearby include the Thunder Swamp Trail (Hike 45) and Big Bear Swamp (Hike 43). For a free trail map of the Thunder Swamp Trail System, write to Delaware State Forest, HC 1, Box 95A, Swiftwater, PA 18370-9723; or call 570-895-4000.

42

Bruce Lake Natural Area

Location: Between Promised Land State Park and I-84

Distance: 11.8 km (7.4 miles)

Time: 3½ hours

Vertical rise: 98 meters (320 feet)

Highlights: Glacial lake

Maps: USGS 7½' Promised Land; park map

The Bruce Lake Natural Area in the Delaware State Forest is just north of Promised Land State Park. It contains a glacial lake and several swamps. It is a sample of northern New England and Canada set in the Mid-Atlantic states.

Bruce Lake itself has no cottages, no roads, no outboard motors, and—unless you carry one in—no boats. Yes, Ontario has 250,000 lakes, but this one is ours. The trails are blue-blazed and have good footing.

If you stuck to the old roads now reverting to trails, you could get by with walking shoes, but this hike includes a circuit of Bruce Lake itself, where your boots will help with the rocks.

How to Get There

There are two access points to the Bruce Lake Natural Area along PA 390. This hike uses the northern one, which is just 0.1 mile south of exit 26 off I-84. The Egypt Meadows parking area is on your left.

The Trail

Pass the gate on blue-blazed Egypt Meadows Road and head into the woods, passing a trail register and a carsonite trail sign. Land managers are enamored of carsonite posts, but I find them lacking in aesthetic value compared to the old-fashioned wooden sign. We'll see what they look like in 10 years; already some of the decals are flaking off. After even 20 years, a well-made routed wooden sign may look a bit scruffy, but it will still be perfectly legible.

Next, pass the Snow Shoe Trail on your right and then a small swamp to your left. At 400 meters turn right onto Panther Swamp Road. Then bear right at a junction with the blue-blazed Egypt Meadows Trail, which provides a way to vary your return (see the map). Egypt Meadows Lake, formed by a dam built by the Civilian Conservation Corps, can be seen through the trees.

Panther Swamp Road passes over a low hill. Note the sheep laurel growing along this section. Panther Swamp is visible to your right.

Turn left onto Bruce Lake Road at 1.4 km. The small bridge visible to your right crosses the outlet from Panther Swamp. Next, you pass the other end of Egypt Meadows Trail, then reach a bridge across the narrows of Egypt Meadows Lake. On my last visit I found water flowing across the approach to the bridge. There had just been a lot of rain, and I thought little of it until I noticed that the lake levels were different above and below the bridge. Peering under the bridge on the high side, I couldn't see a thing—the water level was up to the bottom of the bridge. But from the low side I found that beavers had built their dam under the bridge, raising the level of the southern part of Egypt Meadows Lake by half a meter! These animals have produced a pond of unusual size.

Continue east on Bruce Lake Road, passing witch hazel bushes. This shrub blooms in fall, starting in September and continuing after all its leaves have fallen and the snow is flying.

Beyond, you can see a low cliff through the trees with a large white pine growing in the scant layer of soil on top. This cliff was produced by a glacier "plucking" blocks of rock from the "downstream" side of the ledge. The rock froze to the moving ice and broke off along bedding planes and joints as the glacier moved.

At 3.9 km you reach the junction with the West Branch of the Bruce Lake Trail on your right. Camping is no longer permitted at Bruce Lake. Continue ahead and you'll see Bruce Lake between the trees. There are a number of side trails leading to the lakeshore.

Look for a patch of bedrock near the north end of the lake. It is marked with scratches called glacial striations, which show the direction of motion of the ice and were caused by rocks frozen in the bottom of the ice sheet. Here at Bruce Lake the ice may have been a kilometer in depth, but it moved only centimeters per day.

The bedrock is exposed here now because the soil was burned off by forest fires after the region was logged. If the bedrock had not been protected by the soil, the striations would have weathered away thousands of years ago.

Continue east on the old road, passing a junction with an unmarked trail. The Bruce Lake Trail swings around to the south and passes a disabled water pump. Beyond, the East Branch of the Bruce Lake Trail narrows to a real trail. At one time this trail was blazed yellow; it has been reblazed blue, but a few of the old yellow blazes survive. The footway is excellent. It is far enough back from the lake to stay dry and relatively free of rocks.

On a recent visit I had to stop suddenly in my tracks to watch a buck with a magnificent rack bound across the trail in front of me. I had been moving upwind, so he didn't smell or hear my approach.

The southern part of the lake becomes a swamp and the trail continues south on higher ground before edging to the west. At 6.3 km you reach a short but welcome bridge over the outlet from Bruce Lake. Just beyond is the junction with the West Branch Trail.

You could extend your hike here by turning left and following the Bruce Lake, Rock Oak, and Brown Trails encircling Balsam Swamp.

However, on this hike you turn right onto the West Branch and follow it back to Bruce Lake Road. The West Branch is rockier than the East and has a couple of wet spots. Turn left onto Bruce Lake Road and retrace your steps to the bridge over the Egypt Meadows Lake narrows. Just beyond, you could vary your return by turning right onto the Egypt Meadows Trail. Otherwise, retrace your steps via the Panther Swamp Trail to your car on PA 390.

Other hiking opportunities can be found at Promised Land State Park (Hike 44) and on the Blooming Grove Trail System (Hike 34) north of exit 30 off PA 402.

43

Big Bear Swamp

Location: East of PA 402,
north of Stroudsburg

Distance: 14.2 km (8.8 miles)

Time: 5¼ hours

Vertical rise: 220 meters (730 feet)

Highlights: Natural area

Maps: USGS 7½' Twelvemile Pond, Lake
Maskenozha; Thunder Swamp Trail
System map

The Thunder Swamp Trail System in the Delaware State Forest was built by the Youth Conservation Corps (YCC) in the 1970s. It covers a variety of terrain in the Poconos, from dry ridges to swamps, wetlands, and streams. Actually, there is no Thunder Swamp, but the YCC members liked the name.

Routine maintenance is performed by state forest workers and volunteers from the Pocono Outdoor Club. Rectangular blazes are used to mark the trails—orange for the main trail, red for side trails. Most intersections are marked with trail signs, many of which were made by Keystone Trails Association volunteers and installed during an April 1991 expedition.

Public lands in the Poconos are contorted into gerrymanders. At various places the trails must thread narrow corridors of public land or take circuitous detours to avoid private land.

The many swamps in the Poconos result from the glaciation of the area 15,000 to 20,000 years ago. Preglacial valleys were blocked with glacial debris, so many areas were poorly drained. The swamps today are filled with rhododendron and black spruce, making them all but impenetrable to humans, but providing a refuge for bears. The bear population in the Poconos is the most secure of all regions in the state. Human residents of the Poconos seem to get on fairly well with the bears, even when one is hibernating under their deck. You aren't guaranteed of seeing bears on this hike—but they will know you are here.

People aren't the only creatures who use trails; so do bears, deer, and coyotes. Look for their scat along the trails. Coyote and fox scat will frequently be deposited on top of a rock to say, "This is my trail."

Big Bear Swamp, the site of this hike, is located in the Stillwater Natural Area. The 780 hectares were logged and burned before they became state forest.

Rocks grow wild in the Poconos with their hard, sharp ends up, and wet spots are plentiful; wear your hiking boots.

How to Get There

The trailhead is a parking lot on Flat Ridge Road. It can be reached from exit 30 off I-84 by driving south on PA 402 for 10.6 miles. Then turn left onto paved Old Bushkill Road (SR 2003) and drive 1.6 miles. Turn left onto gravel Flat Ridge Road and continue for 2.2 miles to the parking area on your right.

The trailhead can also be reached from exit 309 off I-80. Follow US 209 north to Marshalls Creek and turn north onto PA 402. Continue on PA 402 to Old Bushkill Road, at the Burnt Mills trailhead. Finally, you can reach it from the blinker on US 209 in Bushkill by turning north onto Old Bushkill Road.

The Trail

Start your hike by heading down the red-blazed trail at the edge of the parking lot. Soon you pass a trail register.

At 170 meters, keep left for the Stillwater Natural Area. The trail circles Painter Swamp. The name probably refers to *Felis concolor*, the mountain lion, or panther. Spruces and large white pines, together with highbush blueberries—a favorite summer food of bears—grow along the trail. Also look for sheep laurel.

At 1.1 km you reach the corner of a dam that has raised the water level in Painter

Swamp to form a pond. Jog left 20 meters on a jeep road and continue on the red-blazed trail to a junction at 1.4 km. Turn left onto the orange-blazed main trail here. Shortly, the trail jogs right for 45 meters before continuing. Watch the blazes carefully here.

Cross Coon Swamp Road at 2.2 km. There is a junction with a red-blazed trail that makes a loop through the northern part of the Stillwater Natural Area, returning to the orange-marked trail at 2.9 km. This loop is not included in this hike, but it is an option; it would add about 4 km to your total distance. For this hike, though, follow the orange blazes and, at 3.1 km, cross a bridge over Little Bush Kill Creek. Next, the trail picks up an old woods road through mountain laurel. Follow it to 3.8 km, where you turn left on trail. (Ahead, the old road would cross a corner of private land.)

Cross a stream on rocks and continue to an unsigned trail junction at 4.2 km. Here the orange blazes go in both directions in order to circle Big Bear Swamp. Turn left onto the woods road and follow it past the first of many rock ledges around the swamp. At 4.8 km turn right on trail, passing white pines and black spruces.

Turn left at 6.5 km past hemlocks and more spruces. Look for painted trilliums here in May. Then cross a log bridge. There are some stone steps at 7.4 km. Look for bear scat around the borders of the swamp.

If you wish to enter the swamp, be prepared to get your feet wet, and be ab-solutely sure to take your compass. It is very easy to go around in circles.

At 9.1 km, turn right onto the old woods road you followed earlier. Soon you reach a heavily posted border of private land. Cross the outlet from Big Bear Swamp at 9.8 km. You can either rock-hop on the old road or detour downstream to a bridge.

At 10 km you close the loop around Big Bear Swamp. Note the three blazes on a rock in the trail. Turn left and retrace your steps to the bridge over Little Bush Kill. About 1.5 km of the creek meander through state forest land. These are the "stillwaters" of the natural area's name.

Continue to retrace your steps to the junction of orange- and red-marked trails at 12.8 km. Turn right on the red and follow the blazes carefully, avoiding a trail that climbs the hill.

At the edge of Painter Swamp, turn left and walk across the dam. See where it washed out and was rebuilt by beavers. Part of this section is bridged, but the rest can be very wet in high water. The far side of the dam affords the best views of Painter Swamp.

At 13.3 km turn right at a signed junction of red-blazed trails. Pass a campsite and continue to 14.1 km, another junction of red-blazed trails. Turn left to return to the parking lot on Flat Ridge Road.

The Thunder Swamp Trail System offers many additional hiking opportunities; see Hikes 41 and 45.

44

Promised Land State Park

Location: South of exit 26 off I-84

Distance: 14.2 km (8.8 miles)

Time: 4¾ hours

Vertical rise: 110 meters (360 feet)

Highlights: Lake, evergreens

Maps: USGS 7½' Promised Land; Promised Land Trail System map

Promised Land State Park, in the heart of the Poconos, was opened to the public in 1905. However, many of the park's facilities were not built until Civilian Conservation Corps (CCC) manpower became available in the Great Depression. From May 1933 until July 1941, Promised Land State Park was also known as Camp Pocono and Camp S-139. A company of the CCC was established in the present Deerfield and Pickerel Point Campgrounds.

Many worthwhile conservation and recreational projects were carried out during these years. The CCC men built fire roads and trails, reforested the terrain, established campgrounds (more than 500 sites are now available in four campgrounds), and built picnic pavilions and bathhouses. In addition, they built 12 rustic cabins still in use on Bear Wallow Road.

If you look around the park, you can find more evidence of the CCC era. The park museum, too, contains photographs and artifacts.

The *Promised Land* name was bestowed sarcastically by Shakers who had been promised riches from the wilderness. When they arrived in 1878, they found the ground filled with rocks and boulders. They soon departed, leaving only the name.

You will want your hiking boots for this long trail, with its many rocks and wet areas. All the trails in the park are blazed blue. If you see paint blazes of other colors, ignore them.

How to Get There

Promised Land can be reached from exit 26 off I-84. Drive south on PA 390 for 2.9

miles. Then turn left onto North Shore Road and go 0.3 mile to a small parking area on the left side of the road.

The Trail

Head into the woods on the Rock Oak Ridge Trail, a woods road. Cross an intermittent stream and reach a junction with the Boundary Trail. This junction, like others in the park, is marked with carsonite posts bearing the names of the trails, icons identifying permissible users (hikers, snowmobilers, horses, and so on), and various numbers. Every trail junction in Promised Land and Bruce Lake Natural Area has been numbered as shown on the map of the Promised Land Trail System. The number of each junction is indicated at the top of a carsonite post. Arrows farther down the post, point in the directions of the next intersections on each trail. Note the sheep laurel growing near this junction. Its pink

Promised Land Lake

flowers blooming in spring are much smaller than those of the more familiar mountain laurel, which you soon pass through as well.

Continue at 1 km on the Telephone Trail, which follows the path of a former telephone line, leaving the woods road behind. (The Telephone Trail is very rocky. You can avoid it by continuing on the Rock Oak Ridge Trail, then turning right onto the Bruce Lake Trail—but at the cost of lengthening your hike.) Next, pass a peat bog to the left of the trail and reach a junction with the Whittaker Trail. At 2.5 km jump from rock to rock as the trail crosses a woodland pool amid highbush blueberry.

Turn right onto the Bruce Lake Trail at 2.9 km. This trail has a much better footway, courtesy of the CCC. Soon you reach a section of evergreens: hemlocks first, then white pines, spruces, and rhododendrons. Next, cross a footbridge over Big Inlet and turn right onto the Big Inlet Trail—actually a

gated woods road. This trail is also known as the Lake Laura Road.

At 5.7 km you reach another junction with the Boundary Trail. This trail could be used to avoid the road walking that lies ahead, but it is poorly marked and unmaintained. So proceed to paved North Shore Road at 5.9 km and turn left. Here there are larch and spruce trees, and views of Promised Land Lake.

Just before crossing Burley Inlet, you will spot the Short Trail to your left; ignore it. Turn left at 7.5 km onto the Burley Inlet Trail. Keep left at a junction of woods roads to reach yet another Boundary Trail junction. Continue ahead on the Burley Inlet Trail, passing a junction with the Snow Shanty Trail at 9.4 km. Then pass through a clearing and continue to a gate. Turn right just beyond to reach a junction with the Rhododendron Trail, a snowmobile trail in-season. It is marked with orange diamonds nailed to the trees.

The Poconos

At 10.5 km cross Pickerel Point Road. The park office and a public telephone are on the far side of PA 390. The Rhododendron Trail, often lined with dense stands of this shrub, continues north between Promised Land Lake to your right and PA 390 to your left. It passes a white pine plantation just before crossing Park Avenue at 12.8 km. The trail passes between several cottages at this point.

Walk behind the boat rental (outhouses to your right) and cross the dam forming Promised Land Lake at 13.2 km. The route, without benefit of blazes, becomes more difficult to follow beyond, but head between the picnic area and swimming beach to a paved parking lot. At the far end follow a gated but paved old road that leads to the Pines Campground. Continue to the far end of the campground and turn right onto the access road. In just 15 meters turn right onto an unmarked old gravel road. This converges quickly with North Shore Road, just across from your car.

There are many other hiking opportunities at Promised Land, ranging from the 1.5 km Conservation Trail, to all-day hikes in the Bruce Lake Natural Area to the north (see Hike 42), to an extensive system of trails west of PA 390. Promised Land has 50 km of trails. If you are looking for trails, not farmland, this truly is a Promised Land in the Poconos.

45

Thunder Swamp Trail

Location: On PA 402 north of Stroudsburg

Distance: 15.1 km (9.4 miles)

Time: 5¼ hours

Vertical rise: 250 meters (820 feet)

Highlights: Cascades

Maps: USGS 7½' Twelvemile Pond; Thunder Swamp Trail System map

The Thunder Swamp Trail in Delaware State Forest is one of the gems of the Poconos. Actually, there is no Thunder Swamp; the Youth Conservation Corps crew that opened the trail back in the 1970s liked the name. The trail system itself has a main loop centered on PA 402, along with additional side trails and loops.

The Pocono Plateau was heavily glaciated, so it contains many natural lakes, ponds, bogs, rapids, and waterfalls; other lakes have been created by dams. Glaciation scrambles the drainage patterns of a region.

The Delaware State Forest consists of 29,000 hectares in Pike, Monroe, and Carbon Counties. There are many housing developments in Pike County. These are first, not second, homes, in many cases, because Times Square is only 90 minutes away. The Thunder Swamp Trail is one of the features that people fled the city to find.

You will want your boots for this rocky trail, which has streams to cross and many wet spots.

How to Get There

This is a car-shuttle hike. To drop off your first car, take exit 30 off I-84. Drive south on PA 402 for 10.9 miles to the Burnt Mills parking area on the east side of the road. Leave one car here. Then continue south for 6.1 miles to Thunder Swamp trailhead parking, also on the east side of PA 402.

To reach the Thunder Swamp Trail from I-80, drive north on US 209 to Marshalls Creek, then take PA 402 north.

TST = Thunder Swamp Trail

The Trail

Head into the woods, following orange paint blazes, from the north end of the parking area. Immediately the trail enters from west of PA 402 and you pass a trail register. The trail continues through an open forest of oaks and maples; farther on, you cross a stream on rocks. At 1.3 km turn left at a junction with a trail that used to be red-blazed and that returns to PA 402.

Cross the stream again and continue to Saw Creek. There is a junction with a red-blazed trail at 2.1 km. At 2.2 km cross Saw Creek on a footbridge built by Keystone Trails Association volunteers back in October 1986.

Now move upstream along Red Rock Run. There are many small cascades, then a large one at 2.5 km. Cross a power-line swath and continue upstream.

At 4.5 km turn left onto a woods road and leave the run behind. Shagbark hickory grows here, as does highbush blueberry. Next, turn right at a junction of woods roads and climb. Bear right where the roads come together and walk among some pitch pines.

This route passes stands of witch hazel, a shrub that blooms in fall. The yellow flowers look like those of forsythia, only there generally aren't as many. Witch hazel may continue to flower until the snow flies.

Bear left on Red Rock Run Road at 6.6 km, pass a log landing to the right, and turn right onto a trail. It climbs a low ridge and, at 8.7 km, crosses an intermittent stream. Then it crosses an old stone wall—no shortage of building material here. Did some optimist try to farm this land?

At 8.9 km you come to a confusing section. Turn left onto a woods road, then left again where there are no blazes (due to a shortage of large trees). The blazes soon start up again, though, and you bear right on trail. Pass a pond to your left, then through a no-cut buffer between two clear-cuts. Cross an intermittent stream, followed by Whittaker Road with its power line at 10.2 km.

Cross another stream and climb to where you can see Lake Minisink through the trees. Walk along the edge of a cliff to a junction of orange-blazed trails at 12.3 km. Turn left on a forestry road toward Saw Creek. (To your right, an orange-blazed trail leads to the Stillwater Natural Area.)

At 13.4 km the orange blazes turn left again along Saw Creek. Continue ahead on a road bridge over Saw Creek; this route is red-blazed. Pass over a stream in a culvert and gradually climb to a vehicle gate at 15 km. The Burnt Mills parking lot is just beyond.

Additional hiking can be found at the nearby Big Bear Swamp (Hike 43) and Pennel Run (Hike 41) Natural Areas, as well as along other parts of the Thunder Swamp Trail System.

46

Painter Creek Loop

Location: 12 miles east of Wilkes-Barre

Distance: 15.6 km (9.7 miles)

Time: 5¼ hours

Vertical rise: 280 meters (920 feet)

Highlights: Pinchot Trail, view, mountain bogs and stream

Maps: USGS 7½' Thornhurst, Pleasant View Summit, Avoca, Moscow; Pinchot Trail map

The Lackawanna State Forest is one of Pennsylvania's smaller state forests, with only 3,300 hectares divided into two tracts, one on each side of the North Branch of the Susquehanna River. This circuit hike is in the Thornhurst tract, east of Wilkes-Barre on the Pocono Plateau.

The Pinchot Trail was built by the Northeast Group of the Sierra Club but is now managed and maintained by the Pennsylvania Bureau of Forestry. The trail is named for Gifford Pinchot, first chief of the USDA Forest Service, twice governor of Pennsylvania, and America's first professional forester. (See Hike 6 for more information on Gifford Pinchot.)

There is a lot of good footway on the Pinchot Trail, but there are also some rocks and wet areas, so wearing your boots is advisable for this hike.

How to Get There

Despite its proximity to Wilkes-Barre, the trailhead on Bear Lake Road is difficult to find. From the east it can be reached from exit 13 off I-380. Turn north onto PA 435 at a confusing (and dangerous) junction at a red blinker. Avoid taking I-380 west. Drive north for 1.5 miles and turn left at a yellow blinker. A sign says THORNHURST 7 MILES. This is SR 2013, also known as River Road. Follow River Road for 5.9 miles, then turn right onto Pine Grove Road and drive 1.5 miles to a stop sign. Turn right onto Bear Lake Road (SR 2016) and follow it for 2.5 miles to the Pinchot trailhead.

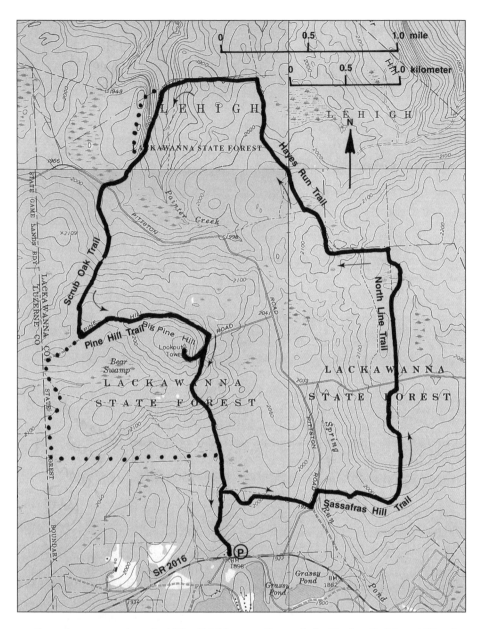

From the west, take exit 178 off I-81. Avoid the airport and drive west on PA 315 to the second traffic light in Dupont (1.1 miles). Then turn left on Suscon Road and drive about 12 miles to the trailhead.

To reach the Pinchot Trail from I-80, take exit 284 and drive north on PA 115 toward Wilkes-Barre. It is 4.6 miles from the traffic light in Blakeslee (the junction is with PA 940) to a paved road, SR 2040 (which will change to SR 2013 at the county line). Turn right and drive 5.1 miles to a junction with Bear Lake Road (SR 2016). Turn left and drive 4.3 miles to the trailhead.

The Trail

Follow the orange blazes into the woods on stepping-stones. This is the Powder Magazine Trail. At a well-made trail register, sign in. Trail maps may be available here. Next, pass sheep laurel, mountain laurel, and highbush blueberry (ripe in July). The berry picker on the other side of the bush may be a bear. Then pass a notable shad tree; most shadbushes never get this big. Black gum and gray birch also grow along the trail.

At 700 meters pass a junction with the red-blazed Pine Hill Trail, on which you will return. Cross a stream on rocks and note the tamarack growing in the acid soil. Jog left 120 meters on Pittston Road, then continue on the Sassafras Hill Trail. Cross a spring area and turn right briefly before resuming your easterly course. In May look for painted trilliums—and, yes, sassafras trees really do grow here.

Turn left at 2.7 km to head straight north. Next, make a brief excursion to the west, returning to your northerly course at Sassafras Road. There is a parking area to your right.

Continue on a grassy swath along the North Line Trail to a "permanent herbaceous opening," which is jargon for wildlife food. Note the fruit trees planted in plastic tubes. The tubes keep deer from eating the trees until they get big and tough. Solar ultraviolet will degrade the plastic tubes after some years.

Continue north on trail through birch trees. A path this straight must have once been a fire lane or an old boundary line. The footway is excellent. Climb a bedrock ledge

and bear right past a small swamp. Turn left onto the Spruce Hill Trail at 5.2 km.

At 5.5 km there is a wet meadow of wild azaleas to your left. In May they form a fuchsia expanse—though wild azalea is usually pink. The trail turns rough and rocky until 6.1 km, where you proceed on a woods road. Then turn right onto a trail, which is probably Hayes Run; there is a post but no sign at this junction.

Pass pitch pines as you follow a grassy footway. At 7.7 km turn left onto the Painter Creek Trail along the state forest boundary—white blazes. Then cross a seep area (a diffuse spring, and important for wildlife survival in winter) and descend steeply. Cross an old road, then Painter Run on a log bridge. Painter Run is shaded by hemlock and spruce.

At 8.6 km turn left onto a red-blazed trail for a gentler climb. The trail soon passes an old logging railroad grade; you can see where the ties rotted in place. Ties were not treated with creosote, so they lasted only a few years and were not reused.

Rejoin the main trail at 9.4 km. Jog left around a swampy area and continue to Pittston Road at 9.7 km. Proceed on the Scrub Oak Trail and continue to climb. Toward the top, scrub oaks really do grow along the trail. The presence of this species indicates some of the poorest soil in the state.

Turn left onto the red-blazed Pine Hill Trail—actually an old grassy road—at 11.4 km. Avoid another trail to your right and continue to a steel gate. Turn right onto a rough trail that passes a massive ledge to the right. At 12.9 km turn right onto a gravel road and climb to Pine Hill Vista. A tower has been built here to get you above the trees and permit a 360-degree view.

To the south you can see Bear Lake, but for the most part the Poconos form a plateau. To the north you look across the Wyoming Valley to North Mountain on the horizon. Wilkes-Barre and Scranton are hidden in the Wyoming Valley. There is usually a good breeze at the top of the tower.

Head back down the road but turn right onto the Pine Hill Trail. Pass through a stand of sassafras, then cross a grassy swath. The red-blazed Frank Gantz Trail comes in from the right at 14.4 km. Frank Gantz is the retired truck driver who laid out the Pinchot Trail, as well as trails at nearby Tobyhanna and Gouldsboro State Parks. He explored the forest on foot, finding old trails and grades as well as new routes and deciding just where the trail should go. The trail between the two parks is also named for him. Without such dedicated volunteers, hiking in our state would be impoverished.

Continue past a spruce plantation on the left to Powder Magazine Trail. Turn right on the orange blazes and retrace your steps to the parking lot.

More hiking opportunities in Lackawanna State Forest are found on the Pinchot Trail System; see Choke Creek Trail (Hike 39). Other loops are also possible along the blazed trails and low-use forestry roads.

47

Fourth Run Loop

Location: *Hickory Run State Park, near the junction of I-80 and I-476*

Distance: *20.0 km (12.4 miles)*

Time: *6 hours*

Vertical rise: *285 meters (940 feet)*

Highlights: *Mountain streams*

Maps: *USGS 7½' Hickory Run; park map*

This circuit hike makes a grand tour of the extensive trail system at Hickory Run State Park. Although you will only use four trails, you will intersect five others along the way.

Of course there are rocks and wet spots, some of them very wet, so you will want your hiking boots. Bicycles are prohibited on trails at Hickory Run.

How to Get There
The trailhead is a parking area on the south side of PA 534, about 0.1 mile before the park office. Hickory Run State Park is reached from exit 274 off I-80. Follow PA 534 east; this road traverses the park. See Hike 40 for more detailed directions to Hickory Run State Park.

The Trail
Start your hike by crossing PA 534 and starting up the paved road. Cross a bridge over Hickory Run and continue ahead at a road junction, passing a piped spring. Bear left on the Fourth Run Trail at 0.5 km and immediately pass the Shades of Death Trail, which diverges to your right. Cross one pole line, then a second. The trail returns to the second pole line and follows it.

At 1 km the Manor House Trail diverges left. Most (but not all) trail junctions along this hike are signed. At 1.2 km bear right away from the pole line, but return to it at 1.8 km. The pole-line swath is filled with highbush blueberry (ripens in July) and mountain laurel (blooms in June). Cross a stream at 2.7 km where the trail swings back into the woods.

Bear left at 3 km where the Stage Trail comes in from your right, leaving the pole line for good. Rhododendron (blooms in July), birch, and sheep laurel grow along the trail. Sheep laurel blooms at the same time as mountain laurel, but has deep pink flowers.

Cross Fourth Run on rocks at 4.7 km and proceed to a junction with the Bear Trail. Turn right onto the Fourth Run Trail and follow it to a culvert under I-476. Here Fourth Run and the Fourth Run Trail become indistinguishable.

Mountain laurel

On the far side, the trail returns to its original alignment, which was blocked by the construction of the turnpike. At 7.2 km cross Fourth Run for the last time and continue along the well-posted boundary of private land. Soon the trail bears right, reaching Boulder Field Road at 8.3 km.

Continue straight ahead on Boulder Field Road and cross a bridge over Hickory Run. Follow the road as it turns right at the junction with the Stage Trail and then passes under I-476. Just beyond the underpass, turn left, then right, on the Gamewire Trail, which follows the boundary of a game reserve created by General Harry C. Trexler. After logging ended in this area, Trexler bought most of what is now the park at tax sales.

This trail has a good footway, but after a gentle descent it becomes very wet. Enter a meadow at 15.2 km, then reach a picnic area with tables, a drinking fountain, and rest rooms. There is a trail sign at this end of the Gamewire Trail. Keep right along the edge of the woods to find a pole line at the far side of the picnic area. Follow the line, then pick up a woods road that leads to a footbridge over Sand Spring Run.

On the other side bear left, passing playground equipment, to a gravel service road. Follow this road along the edge of woods, through the day-use area, past the concession stand and beach. Continue beyond the dam out to PA 534 at 17.1 km.

Turn left onto PA 534 and cross the one-lane bridge over Sand Spring Run. Just after the bridge, turn right onto the Beach Trail at the end of the guide rail. Ignore a trail to the right and continue past the corner of a meadow. Walk straight ahead on road at campground site 152; bear right on trail at site 158. The Beach Trail is used by campers to reach the swimming area.

At the next loop of the campground, turn left on road between sites 52 and 53.

Proceed to the paved road and turn right. At 17.9 km turn left onto the Sand Spring Trail, which is marked with occasional blue diamonds. Cross a stream on rocks and bear left at a fork in the trail. The Blue Trail goes left at 18.4 km. Next, bear right along a rhododendron-banked stream to reach a trail junction at 19.7 km.

At the end of the switchback, continue ahead to the end of a paved road. Pass the park's sewage treatment plant and some service buildings. Cross a bridge over Sand Spring Run and you are back at your car.

See Hikes 31, 33, and 40 for additional hiking opportunities at Hickory Run State Park.

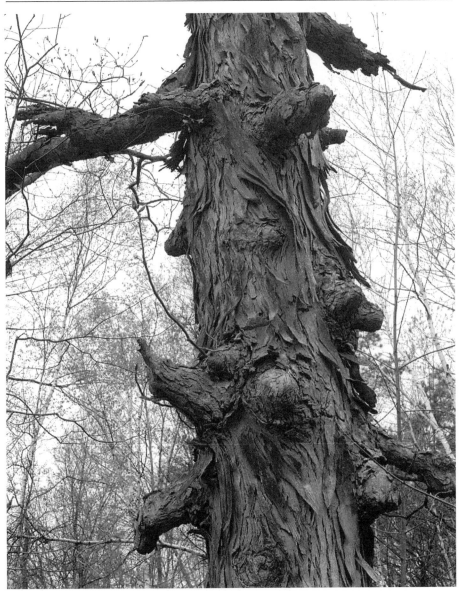

Shagbark hickory

48

Frances Slocum

Location: 10 miles northwest of Wilkes-Barre

Distance: 5.3 km (3.3 miles)

Time: 2 hours

Vertical rise: 67 meters (220 feet)

Highlights: Hemlock glen, stream, meadow, lake

Maps: USGS 7½' Kingston; park map

Frances Slocum State Park, the only Pennsylvania park named for a female, honors a girl who was kidnapped by Native Americans from nearby Wilkes-Barre in 1778, when she was only 5 years old. Her first night in captivity was spent under a rock ledge—now within the park and visited on the Frances Slocum Trail. She tried to escape that night but was recaptured and grew up among the Native Americans. Mocanaquah, as they called her, was twice married to chieftains and had several children. Fifty years later, when her brothers were finally able to locate her, she refused to leave and chose to live out her life on a reservation in Indiana.

You may want your boots for this short hike, as there are many wet areas, at least in spring. The trails at Frances Slocum were built and are maintained by volunteers from the Susquehanna Trailers Hiking Club.

How to Get There

The park is located only 10 miles from Wilkes-Barre, but it is challenging to find. From Trucksville on PA 309, turn onto Carverton Road at a sign for the park; follow signs along Carverton Road for a total of 6.8 miles, to Eighth Street. Turn left onto Eighth, then left again onto Mount Olivett Road. Make another left at the park's main entrance and follow this road to a T-junction. Turn right and park on your left just before the boat mooring, a distance of 1 mile from the entrance. This is as close as you can park to the visitors center, where the Deer Trail starts.

The Trail

Head down the closed road to the visitors center. Here you can borrow a guide to the Deer Trail. Please return it when you finish your hike. The Field Notes will explain some of the habitats and their residents you may see along the way.

Continue behind the visitors center to find the first blazes; this section takes you along the lakeshore. The first yellow blazes are 175 meters beyond the center. They measure 5 by 15 cm in size and are painted on trees, posts, rocks, and even the pavement of an old road. Variations of the Deer

Trail have a diagonal black stripe across their blazes. If you follow one type of blaze on the way out, you can vary your return by following the other on the way back.

Beware of unblazed trails along the Deer Trail. They appear to have been worn by mountain bikes and are not shown on the park map.

The plain yellow blazes lead you along a graveled path, which soon becomes dirt or mud in-season. When you enter the hemlocks, look for a black-slash-blazed trail that comes in from your right. This leads to the large parking lots in the middle of the park, but it is shown slightly wrong on the park map. Follow the yellow blazes.

The trail now enters a hemlock glen above a small stream. Descend and cross the stream on rocks, then head downstream. Bear right at the junction with a black-stripe-blazed trail entering from your left.

Next, enter a brushy meadow and bear left. At 1.2 km cross a bridge over Abrahams Creek. Beyond the creek, turn left onto an old paved road. (There is a variation of the trail to your right that circles the bay. I suspect it was used before the artificial stepping-stones were installed along the old road. It appears to be somewhat overgrown now.)

Along the road you soon reach a row of artificial stepping-stones. Take a good look at them. They consist of fire rings that have been filled with concrete, and are the most stable stepping-stones you are likely to find anywhere.

The Deer Trail is well named. You will see many tracks in the wet places and are likely to see the deer themselves. They just stand there and look back at you.

Turn right off the old road at 1.8 km, just before it enters the lake. (Really—the road predated the lake.) Keep right, then bear left at an old stone wall. The woods are filled with such walls, mute testimony to the back-breaking labor required to farm these lands.

Turn right onto another old road between stone walls, then climb a rock outcrop on well-made stone steps. Turn left, then left again to reach a stream. Cross on the ruins of an old dam.

Soon the trail descends to the lakeside and heads back. Look for signs of beaver activity along this shore. Cross two streams on rocks and pass a spring. At 3.4 km turn left onto the old paved road and retrace your steps across the bridge over Abrahams Creek. At 4.3 km bear right following the black-striped blazes and cross a stream on rocks. Then bear right at the plain yellow blazes and return to the visitors center.

Additional hiking opportunities at Frances Slocum include the Lake Shore and Frances Slocum Trails in the main part of the park, and the Larch Tree Trail north of the campground on the far side of the lake.

49

Joe Gmiter

Location: About 6 miles west of
Harveys Lake

Distance: 7.2 km (4.5 miles)

Time: 3¼ hours

Vertical rise: 320 meters (1,050 feet)

Highlights: State Game Lands

Maps: USGS 7½' Noxen;
Joe Gmiter Trails map

The Joe Gmiter Trails are four trails in State Game Lands 57 south of Noxen and west of PA 29. The different trails are marked, in order of increasing length, with red, blue, yellow, and orange metal blazes nailed to trees. The trails are on Sorber Mountain and use many of the same sections.

They were built by the Susquehanna Trailers Hiking Club in honor of Joe Gmiter, who was president of Susquehanna Trailers for many years. State Game Lands 57 is the second largest in the state; Sorber Mountain is an isolated section of it east of Bowman Creek.

Maintenance of these trails has been turned over to a Boy Scout troop. The Game Commission permitted only *one side* of the trees to be marked with painted tin can lids. (This requirement seems to have been relaxed a bit in recent years.) Consequently, all these loops are best hiked in a counterclockwise direction.

The Game Commission does not receive any money from general tax revenue. Its support comes from the sale of hunting licenses and other taxes on hunting supplies. Hikers do not contribute through user fees to the purchase or maintenance of game lands, so permission to build hiking trails on game lands is really quite generous.

Because of this hike's steep hills and many wet spots, wear your hiking boots.

How to Get There

The Joe Gmiter trailhead can be most easily reached from PA 29 at Noxen. Turn north onto Market Street (SR 3002) at the

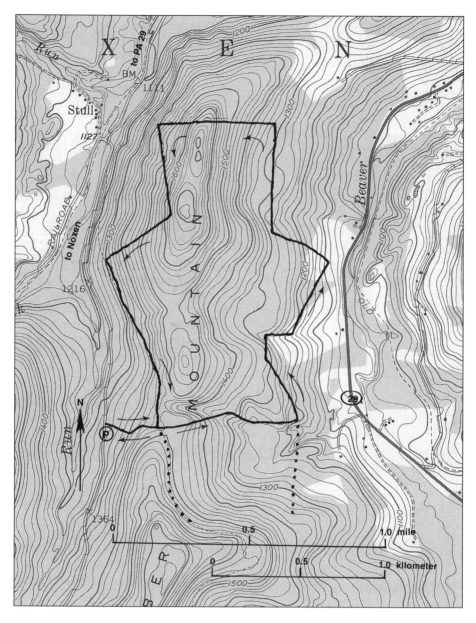

right-angled bend in PA 29. Turn left onto School Street (SR 3002) immediately beyond the bridge over Bowman Creek after just 0.2 mile.

At 2.3 miles, turn left onto Sorber Mountain Road and recross Bowman Creek. This intersection marks the location of the ghost town of Stull, which had a lumber mill. Drive south for 1.2 miles to the game lands parking lot on your left.

The Joe Gmiter trailhead can also be reached from the Ruggles United Methodist

Painted trillium

Church on PA 29. Turn west onto Sorber Mountain Road and drive for 3 miles to the parking lot.

The Trail

At the parking lot there is a large signboard and map showing the routes of the four different trails. They mostly follow the game lands borders, as required by the Game Commission—a prescription that makes for at least one very stiff climb. This hike follows the Yellow Trail, which turns out to be less than its advertised length.

Dodge around the gate and head up the jeep road. Where the jeep road turns right, continue ahead on a grassy road. Note the young forest to your right, resulting from a timber sale.

Reach a major trail junction at 380 meters. The Red Trail comes in from your right; the Orange and Yellow, from your left. Continue ahead on the Yellow Trail. As you start down the hill, note the new growth, mostly aspen and striped maple, on both sides of the trail. At 800 meters you reach the edge of the timber sale.

Turn left at 1 km. Here hemlocks grow along the trail. Cross a stream, noting the hobblebush growing here. The stream can still be seen to your right as you continue.

At 1.4 km you reach another junction: The Blue and Orange Trails come in from your right and the Yellow bears left along the game lands boundary. This boundary is abundantly marked with white paint blazes, and you will follow them for most of this hike. In May, look for painted trilliums here.

Continue on an old woods road to 1.7 km, where you bear left along the game lands boundary. Follow another woods road, then a logging road, crossing several small streams. Turn right to return to the game lands boundary at 2.2 km, where you turn left. Next, turn right at a boundary corner.

At 2.8 km turn left at another corner. Follow an old grade for a bit. Ground cedar and lots of ferns grow along this section. Switchback down to a stream and cross it on rocks at 3.1 km. Note the rubbish heap on adjacent private land. Would we need landfills if our public lands were privatized?

Turn left along the boundary at 3.3 km and climb. Note a red pine growing on adjacent private land. The trail turns right along a more or less level section of the boundary. Listen for the call of the pileated woodpecker: a loud *kikkik-kikkik-kik-kik.* The pileated is a bird of the deep woods.

At 4.1 km turn left and climb. Look for a white or paper birch. The climb becomes very steep near the end. Reach the viewless top, with a stand of hemlocks, at 4.5 km. Then descend to 4.8 km, where you turn left and slab up the side of Sorber Mountain. A jeep road can be seen to the right on private land. Don't take it. It diverges from the boundary, which you follow to 5.4 km.

Turn right and descend steeply. At 5.6 km, where an extra row of white blazes diverges to your right, continue ahead. Reach a trail register at 5.9 km and turn left onto a jeep road that climbs gently. There is a great deal of mountain laurel here. At 6.9 km turn right at the major trail junction and return to your car on Sorber Mountain Road.

The Red, Orange, and Blue Trails on the southern part of Sorber Mountain provide additional hiking opportunities in State Game Lands 57. Maps of the Joe Gmiter Trails can be obtained by writing to Harry West, Box 33-C, Noxen, PA 18636. Please include three first-class stamps.

50

Ricketts Glen

Location: 20 miles west of Wilkes-Barre

Distance: 10.7 km (6.7 miles)

Time: 4½ hours

Vertical rise: 315 meters (1,030 feet)

Highlights: Waterfalls

Maps: USGS 7½' Red Rock; park map

Ricketts Glen is the jewel in the crown of eastern Pennsylvania hiking. It is located on the Allegheny Front in Ricketts Glen State Park, between Williamsport and Wilkes-Barre.

Ricketts Glen is in the glaciated portion of the state. One result of glaciation is the destruction of original drainage patterns when preglacial valleys are blocked or filled. When the glacier recedes, streams cut new valleys. These young valleys are V-shaped and may contain waterfalls—lots of waterfalls. Marcia Bonta, author of *Outbound Journeys in Pennsylvania,* counts 33 waterfalls in Ricketts Glen; the park map identifies only 23.

Ricketts Glen is large by state park standards; it was even proposed as a national park back in the 1930s, although World War II put an end to those plans. The park has more than 5,000 hectares, and adjacent game lands another 34,000. Together they constitute a significantly large tract of wild land.

The park is named for Robert Bruce Ricketts, who rose from private to colonel during the Civil War. Ricketts commanded Battery F at Gettysburg and helped repulse a Confederate attack on July 2, 1863. After the war he acquired vast holdings of virgin timber here, which could not be logged due to the absence of railroads. A railroad was finally built in 1890, and then logging started in earnest. By 1913 the virgin timber had all been cut, and the lumber town of Ricketts became a ghost town.

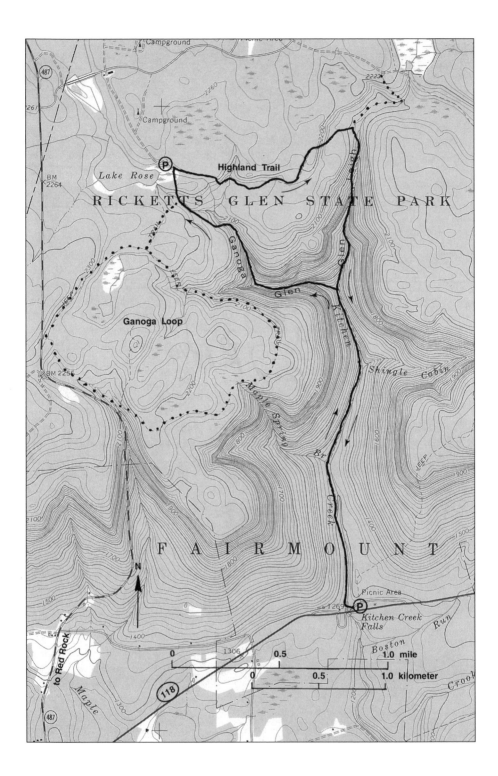

Campground

Picnic Area

2223

2260

2200

2100

P

Lake Rose   **Highland Trail**

R I C K E T T S   G L E N   S T A T E   P A R K

2100   2100

Ganoga   Glen

Glen

Kitchen

2200

2100   Glen

Ganoga Loop

Jeep

1800

BM 2256

Shingle Cabin

Maple Spring

1900

1900

2200   1800   1700

1600

1900

JEEP

1700   900

2100   Br

1600

1500

1500   1400   Creek

1700   F   A   I   R   M   O   U   N   T

N

1600

1500

1400

Picnic Area

P

BM 1269

Kitchen Creek
Falls

to Red Rock

1306

Boston

Run

118

487

Maple

300

Creek

0		0.5		1.0 mile

0		0.5		1.0 kilometer

Harrison Wright Falls, in Ricketts Glen

Curiously, the waterfalls weren't discovered until 1865. Colonel Ricketts hired a crew to build the trail past the falls. It took 28 years of backbreaking labor to complete the trails by 1893. As you will see, these trails require constant maintenance today. Large trees fall across them, steps are carried away by slippage, and bridges are swept away by floods.

Wear good hiking boots for this trip. You will need their traction around the falls. As the trail climbs each falls it is forced into the side of the canyon wall, where seep springs and spray from the cataract keep the rocks wet and the mud liquid. This hike is not advisable for small children, and should be avoided if there is any ice present.

How to Get There

The trailhead for this hike is on PA 118, just 1.6 miles east of its junction with PA 487 in Red Rock. There is a large parking lot on the north side of the highway, just east of the bridge over Kitchen Creek.

The Trail

Head west and find a footbridge over the creek. On the far side, turn right and head upstream. Soon you begin to pass large hemlocks. The timber here was never cut; these trees are centuries old. Cross a bridge over the creek. At 1.3 km return to the west side of Kitchen Creek and continue upstream. Then turn left and climb to a higher grade for a better footway. The two trails are reunited at Murray Reynolds Falls. After this the falls come thick and fast, beginning with Sheldon Reynolds and Harrison Wright.

Reach Watersmeet at 2.7 km. Here Glen Leigh and Ganoga Glen unite. Continue up Ganoga Glen (you will return down Glen Leigh). The next falls is Erie, followed by Tuscarora, Conestoga, and Mohican. Many of the falls are identified with signs—but you may have to look around to find the signs.

The waterfalls are in an enchanted setting with brilliant green moss, multilayered shale, and huge hemlocks leaning over; the smaller falls are as beautiful as the larger, and each unique; some are single cascades, while others have two or three different cascades, one above the other.

Delaware is a good-sized falls, followed by the smaller Seneca Falls. This brings you to Ganoga Falls, which, at 28 meters, is the highest in the park. The trail has to switch back and forth to climb to the top of Ganoga. Note the guard cables at the top. Cayuga and Oneida are of modest size, and are followed by Mohawk.

A shrub growing in the glens is hobblebush, or witch hobble. It blooms in May. Elsewhere in Pennsylvania it has been eaten by the abundant deer herd. It would appear that deer don't frequent these glens, so hobblebush can survive.

At 4.4 km cross a bridge and continue climbing to the Highland Trail, which connects the two glens. Turn right and follow the Highland Trail across a stream. Go through Midway Crevasse at 5.3 km; at 6.3 km turn right onto the Glen Leigh Trail.

Cross a bridge to the far side of Glen Leigh before Onondaga Falls. Note how the bridges are made with locally grown materials—hemlock logs. It would be very difficult to get other construction materials into these narrow valleys.

Onondaga is followed by F. L. Ricketts and Shawnee. Note the large hemlocks growing in the glen. Next comes Huron Falls. Then cross on another bridge. Ozone Falls requires switchbacks, as does R. B. Ricketts. Cross the stream again to reach B. Reynolds, and cross for the last time above Wyandot Falls. Then cross a bridge over Ganoga Glen at Watersmeet. Turn left and retrace your steps to your car.

If you haven't seen enough waterfalls for one day, Adams Falls is just downstream from the PA 118 bridge and can be reached via the Evergreen Trail on the west side of Kitchen Creek.

A shorter version of this hike—only 5.8 km—visits most of the waterfalls. Park at the Rose Lake lot and walk to the junction with the Highland Trail. Then turn right and descend Ganoga Glen. Return via Glen Leigh and the Highland Trail.

There are additional hiking opportunities at Ricketts Glen State Park. If the falls are dried up or icy, try the Ganoga Loop Trail. Avoid the Grand View Loop, however, as the fire tower is fenced off and locked up—so no view.

Index

195, 197
Bruce Lake Trail, 190, 196
Burley Inlet Trail, 196–97
Burnt Mills, 184, 192, 198, 200
Butler Run Trail, 179
Buzzards Trail, 124

C

Cabin Hollow Trail, 100
Caledonia State Park, 26–29, 49
Camelback Mountain, 20, 151–53
Camelback Ski Area, 151, 152
Cameron, James, 37
Camp Michaux, 55
Camp Pocono. *See* Promised Land State Park
camping, overview of, 21–22
Canada geese, 92–94, 118
Capital Area Greenbelt, 72, 73–76
Carlisle, Cumberland Valley, 58–63
Cassel (Isaac) House, 106
Cemetery Ridge, 49, 51
Chamberlain, Joshua Lawrence, 51
Chambersburg, Caledonia State Park, 26–29
Charcoal Hearth Trail (Caledonia State Park), 26–27
charcoal iron furnaces, 26–27, 34, 35, 49, 55, 122
Childs (George W.) Recreation Area, 166, 167–68
Chimney Trail (Susquehannock State Park), 97
Choke Creek Nature Trail, 177–79
Circuit Hikes in Virginia, West Virginia, Maryland, and Pennsylvania, 24
Civil War, 26, 40, 217
    Gettysburg Heritage Trail, 48–53
Civilian Conservation Corps (CCC), 30, 142, 194
Clark Creek, 82, 84
Clarks Ferry Bridge, 77, 80
Clarks Ferry Shelter, 79–80
clothing and equipment, 19, 21
Codorus Creek, 43
Conestoga Trail, 115, 117
Conewago Day-Use Area, 47

Conococheague Creek, 29
Conodoguinet Creek, 59, 63
Conservation Trail, 197
covered bridges, 110, 118–19, 140
coyotes, 32, 192
Crefeld Creek, 109, 110
Cumberland Valley, 58–63
Cumberland Valley Appalachian Trail Management Association, 63
Curtis, William, 24, 48, 49
Cyclorama Center (Gettysburg), 49

D

Dairy Hill Trail, 119, 121
De Hart Dam, 82, 85
Deer Leap Falls, 168
Deer Path Trail (Middle Creek Wildlife Area), 94
deer ticks, 17–18
Deer Trail (Frances Slocum State Park), 210–12
Delaware Canal State Park, 137–41
Delaware River, 141, 162
Delaware State Forest, 21, 198. *See also* Thunder Swamp Trail System
    Blooming Grove Trail System, 22, 158–61, 190
    Bruce Lake Natural Area, 161, 188–90
    camping in, 22
Delaware Water Gap, 16, 152–53
    Mount Minsi, 162–65
Delta Trail, 72
Devil's Den, 49, 51
Diehl House, 105
Dillon, Costa, 24, 48, 49
Dillsburg, 45, 58
Dingmans Falls, 166–68
Dismal Run, 136
Dock, Mira Lloyd, 73
Dock Street Dam, 75, 76
Dunn, Craig, 58

E

Early, Jubal, 26
Easton, Delaware Canal State Park,

M

N

O

P

---

visitors center, 49, 92, 112, 166, 167, 211

Von Steuben, Friedrich, 113

W

Warfield Ridge, 51
Washington Crossing Historical Park, 141
water, drinking, 17, 19
Water Tank Trail, 85
waterfalls
    Dingmans Falls, 166–68
    Hawk Falls, 148–50
    Ricketts Glen, 217–20
Watershed Trail (Kings Gap), 39
Watershed Trail (Nolde Forest), 99, 100
White Clay Creek, 125–29
White Deer Trail, 158, 161
White Oak Picnic Area, 94
White Pine Trail, 119
Whitetail Trail, 67, 69
Wilderness Trail (Tyler Arboretum), 134–36

wildlife. *See also* birdwatching; *and specific wildlife*
    safety tips, 16–18
Wildwood Lake, 70–72
Wilkes-Barre
    Choke Creek Trail, 177–79
    Frances Slocum Trail, 210–12
    Joe Gmiter Trails, 213–16
    Painter Creek Loop, 201–4
    Ricketts Glen, 217–20
Willow Point Trail, 94
Wissahickon Gorge, 107–10
Wissahickon River, 110
Wissler Run, 95, 96, 97
Woodfield Trail (Tyler), 121
Wyandot Falls, 220

Y

Yellow Springs, 81, 84
York. *See also* Gifford Pinchot State Park
    Heritage Trail, 40–43
Young, John, 24
Youth Conservation Corps (YCC), 30, 191, 198